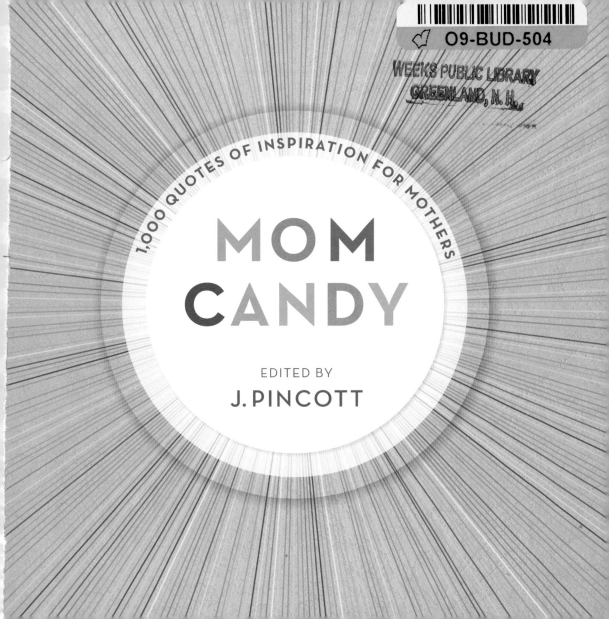

1,000 QUOTES OF INSPIRATION FOR MOTHERS

MOM CANDY

EDITED BY

J. PINCOTT

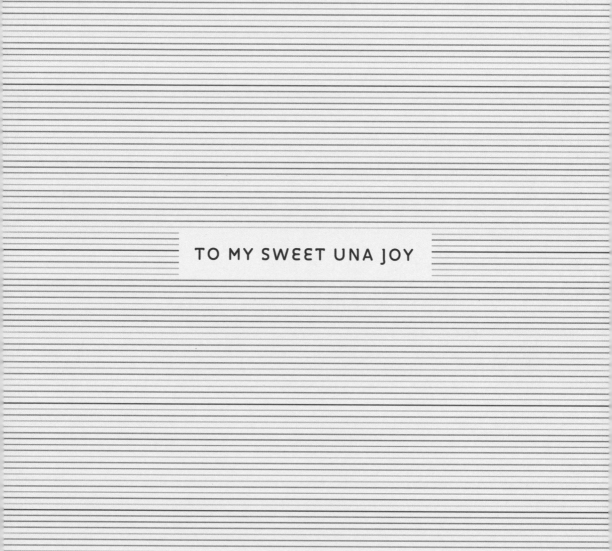

TO MY SWEET UNA JOY

CONTENTS

INTRODUCTION

Sweet and many are the musings about motherhood. *Mom Candy* is a selection of the choicest. One thousand assorted nuggets of parenting insight and inspiration are featured in this book, drawn from interviews, memoirs, poetry, literature, and verse. Many times, I cherry-picked passages as my toddler sat on my lap or nearby on her play rug. I dipped into novels and pored over databases while my daughter turned the pages of her board books. After finding a juicy passage, I'd stop and read to her, then we'd both go back to our respective work. She could see how much I love to read. Looking back, I realize that these were some of our first bonding moments over words and books.

Mom Candy comes in many flavors and textures. Some bits are as light on the tongue and mind as cotton candy (*Children are love made visible. —American proverb*). Others you can really sink your teeth into; they're substantive. (*The simplest gesture, the ephemeral movement, the commonest object all become precious beyond words when touched, noticed, lived by one's own dear child. —Mike Mason).* In the mix are semisweet morsels, too. They are reminders that childhood passes quickly, and to keep our focus on the big picture and not the everyday frustrations (*Think in terms of "the last time"—as in, there will be a last time for everything." —Trisha Ashworth and Amy Nobile).* There are passages that are as decorative and declarative as those inscribed on cakes (*What children take from us, they give. —Sonia Taitz).* The most nourishing contributions put us in the mothering mindset (*The ideal stance is a kind of gentle wonder, now and again brimming over into radical amazement. —Nina Planck).* And then there are the bits that are really sticky; you savor them and they linger. (*The mother and the child always remain joined together with subtle energy, waves, because they go on vibrating on the same wavelength. —Osho, mystic and spiritual teacher).*

A few years ago, before I became a mother, I wouldn't have known much about the range that goes with the role. Now I do. Motherhood is as elastic as taffy; it stretches from the banal to the sublime. Amidst all the nose-wiping, hand-holding, and task-mastering are upwellings of wonder, delight, and overwhelming, awe-inspiring love (*Asking me to describe my son is like asking me to hold the ocean in a paper cup. —Jodi Picoult*). The themes in this collection—from "Bond" and "Release" to "Influence," "Balance," and "Perfection"—attempt to represent some of motherhood's reach and breadth. "Becoming" reminds us of the magical metamorphosis into motherhood. "Gifts" illustrates how those changes improve and enhance our lives. "Time" is a section that I can't read dry-eyed (*I hated going to the playground EVERYDAY. If someone had only told me it wouldn't last forever. —Nancy Woodruff*). Some nuggets can be hard to swallow, but they inspire a mom to live in the moment.

Mom Candy speakers are parents and thinkers of all stripes. Insights come from journalists, actors, CEOs, politicians, teachers, business leaders, poets, psychologists, scientists, and spiritual leaders, among others. First-person quotes from novelists may be drawn from their works of fiction; for full details on these great booksrt and other sources, see the Selected Sources section on page 370.

Mom Candy is a collection of crystallized wisdom. The quotes and passages within channel our thoughts to the best things about being a mother: playfulness and purpose, connection and contentment, laughter and love. They speak to motherhood's ephemeral and eternal joys; of strength, sacrifice, and courage; of limits and life balance; and a mother's infinite value and legacy. Dig into *Mom Candy* when seeking validation or inspiration. Indulge in a quick fix. Graze. Nibble. Binge. Or lift the cover, close your eyes, and just pick one. Motherhood is all about surprise. You never know what you're gonna get.

J. Pincott

BEGINNING

Often one of the biggest treats of motherhood is reminiscing about the early days. There's the pregnancy, which expands body, mind, and soul. Then there's the birth, and baby arrives with all the intensity of a new life. Following that are the unforgettable firsts: the first finger grip, the first smile, the first moment of eye contact. This is all new territory. The terrain is enchanted—with ecstatic heights, eye-misting sights, and the occasional free fall. Looking back, the beginning may feel like it combusted outside of time; those first days have the feel of eternity. Everything is miraculous.

A baby is something you carry inside you for nine months, in your arms for three years and in your heart till the day you die.

—*Mary Mason, writer*

Babies are such a nice way to start people.

—*Don Herold, humorist and writer*

A baby is a blank cheque made payable to the human race.

—*Barbara Christine Seifert*

As we carry our baby inside us, we know almost nothing about it that distinguishes it from anyone else's baby— except that we love it unlike any other baby.

—*Roni Jay, novelist*

Before you were conceived I wanted you.
Before you were born I loved you.
Before you were here an hour I would die for you.
This is the miracle of Mother's love.
—*Maureen Hawkins, actor*

A baby will make love stronger, days shorter, nights longer, bankroll smaller, home happier, clothes shabbier, the past forgotten, and the future worth living for.

—*Anonymous*

Making a decision to have a child—it's momentous. It is to decide forever to have your heart go walking around outside your body.

—*Elizabeth Stone, writer*

Life is always a rich and steady time when you are waiting for something to happen or to hatch.

—*E. B. White, novelist*

A mother's joy begins when new life is stirring inside . . . when a tiny heartbeat is heard for the very first time, and a playful kick reminds her that she is never alone.

—*Anonymous*

I was pregnant with a baby and also with myself, connected by a primordial umbilical cord to other women—to all women past, present, and future: to the female spirit—interested in and needing to be with women more than men for the first time since adolescence.

—*Jane Fonda, actor and activist*

Pregnancy is a kind of miracle. Especially so in that it proves that a man and woman can conspire to force God to create a new soul.

—*Robert Anton Wilson, writer and psychologist*

One of the most exciting things about being pregnant is that I just am accepting the complete unknown; it's a complete mystery and miracle.

—*Natalie Portman, actor*

Pregnancy humbled the husbands. After an initial rush of male pride they quickly recognized the minor role that nature had assigned them in the drama of reproduction, and quietly withdrew into a baffled reserve, catalysts to an explosion they couldn't understand.

—*Jeffrey Eugenides, novelist*

As my pregnancy advanced, I felt a substance was being pumped into my blood that created an almost unquenchable thirst for love; not for more passion or excitement, but for more love in the primal way we experienced love as children: for the love of a parent tucking a child into bed. In short: love as safety and protection.

—*Naomi Wolf, writer, political consultant, and activist*

The life force, the power of Nature, became part of my everyday awareness when I was pregnant. . . . The life force stretched and danced in my body with abandon. Life was no longer something to be gazed at as a spectator gazes at a thunderstorm. I was in the eye of the storm. . . . It was wondrous to feel a part of all that is, to be so intimate with the life force that animates all things.

—Jacqueline Kramer, writer and spiritual teacher

That first pregnancy is a long sea journey to a country where you don't know the language, where land is in sight for such a long time that after a while it's just the horizon—and then one day birds wheel over that dark shape and it's suddenly close, and all you can do is hope like hell that you've had the right shots.

—Emily Perkins, novelist

How you approach birth is intimately connected with how you approach life.

—William Sears, pediatrician

[Pregnancy] provides a sort of malleability. . . . In the same way that the hormone relaxin is making your joints more flexible, your mind is also more open and flexible than when you feel like you've got everything under control.

—*Cassandra Vietan and Sylvia Boorstein, psychologists*

Pregnancy seems designed to prepare you for life as a mother. You start making sacrifices nine months before the child is born, so by the time they put in an appearance you are used to giving things up for them.

—*Brett Kiellerop, writer and life coach*

Birth is as safe as life gets.

—*Harriette Hartigan, birth photographer*

Having a baby is stupendously wonderful, but things may not go as planned. If you have no fixed expectations, nothing can surprise or disappoint you. The ideal stance is a kind of gentle wonder, now and again brimming over into radical amazement, as your story unfolds.

—*Nina Planck, food writer and entrepreneur*

When a woman gives birth her waters break and she pours out the child and the child runs free.

—Jeanette Winterson, novelist

Light flared through every limb, a force far too great to be contained in any human frame; but for that moment she was the Great Mother, giving birth to the world.

—*Marion Zimmer Bradley, novelist*

At four that morning my son, Peter Williams Chambliss, slid into the world tiny and red and roaring with life, and the awful love that caught and whirled me away when they laid him on my stomach was as strong and old as the earth and would, I knew dimly, abide as long. Even as they lifted him out of my arms and I slid finally into sleep, I whispered, "Mine. Mine. Mine."

—*Anne Rivers Siddons, novelist*

In the sheltered simplicity of the first days after a baby is born, one sees again the magical closed circle, the miraculous sense of two people existing only for each other.

—*Anne Morrow Lindbergh, writer, poet, and aviator*

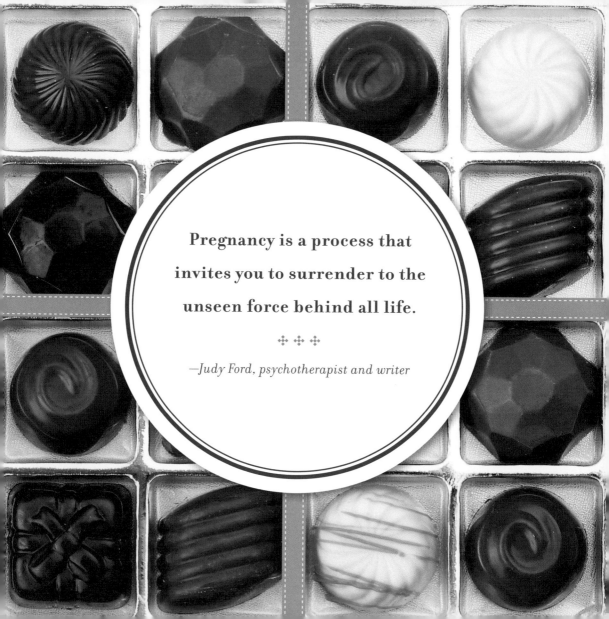

Pregnancy is a process that invites you to surrender to the unseen force behind all life.

✤ ✤ ✤

—*Judy Ford, psychotherapist and writer*

I looked at this tiny perfect creature and it was as though a light switch had been turned on. A giant gush of love flooded out of me.

—Madeleine L'Engle, novelist

A little child born yesterday
A thing on mother's milk and kisses fed.
—Percy Bysshe Shelley, poet

The child must know that he is a miracle, that since the beginning of the world there hasn't been, and until the end of the world there will not be, another child like him.
—Pablo Casals, cellist and conductor

To give life to another being, what a gift! When he finally was placed into my arms, I looked into his precious eyes and felt an overwhelming, unconditional love. . . . I never felt so complete and empowered in my life.

—Gisele Bündchen, model

If one feels the need of something grand, something infinite, something that makes one feel aware of God, one need not go far to find it. I think that I see something deeper, more infinite, more eternal than the ocean in the expression of the eyes of a little baby when it wakes in the morning and coos or laughs because it sees the sun shining on its cradle.

—*Vincent van Gogh, artist*

For nine months I grew a human being inside my belly and then I pushed it out my vagina and now I'm feeding it with my boob. Biology is so . . . weird.

—*Heather Armstrong (Dooce), blogger and entrepreneur*

Do other mothers behold their newborn sons as I did? Do they all find themselves stopped, breathless, in what they were doing to merely stare, in wonder, at the tiny life before them? Do they hold fast to their hungry babies and think fierce thoughts about their futures? Do they draw out a wide circle and say, "Nothing will intrude on this sacred space?"

—*Elizabeth C. Bunce, novelist*

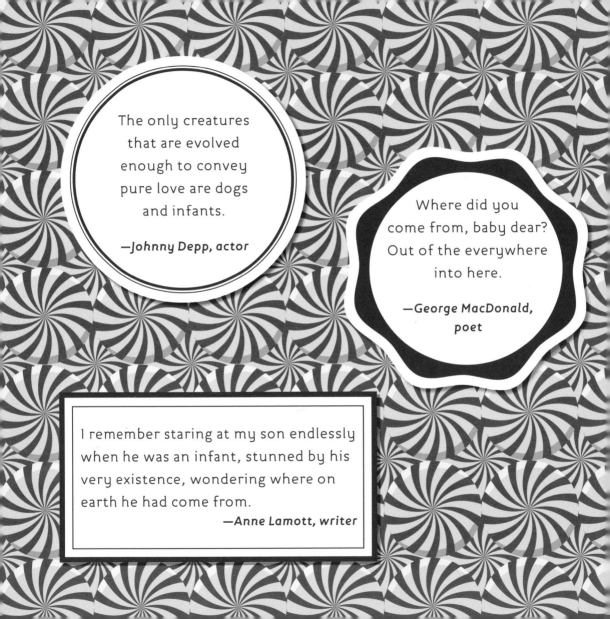

The only creatures that are evolved enough to convey pure love are dogs and infants.

—Johnny Depp, actor

Where did you come from, baby dear? Out of the everywhere into here.

—George MacDonald, poet

I remember staring at my son endlessly when he was an infant, stunned by his very existence, wondering where on earth he had come from.

—Anne Lamott, writer

I had never thought of myself as an especially maternal person, and I was stunned by the intensity of my feelings of love for my firstborn child. I do not remember what I had expected, but his large, round, funny face and bald head and wise old soulful eyes took most of my breath away; I expended the rest by talking to him all night.

—*Lisa Hajeeb Halaby (Queen Noor), queen dowager of Jordan*

The feeling of holding your baby for the first time is magical and filled with spirit. . . . This little bundle of joy who smiles and coos baby sounds at you is a part of you. And it humbles you, for you are in the presence of Love made Flesh.

—*Tommy Chong, novelist*

A new baby is like the beginning of all things—wonder, hope, a dream of possibilities. . . . Babies are almost the only remaining link with nature, with the natural world of living things from which we spring.

—*Eda J. LeShan, writer and psychologist*

Everything we did was a first: first bath, first walk, first drive in the car. It was like we walked into an alternate universe that looked just like the old one, but all the rules were different and we had to relearn how to live.

—*Soleil Moon Frye, actor*

With each spring comes new life, energy and green growth. In summer comes the sun, warm, kind and enduring. Fall brings its canvas of color in careful, gentle change. Winter brews into faithful strength, beauty in pure white. And then comes you. You are all that Nature offers, a blessing, a gift. You are the fifth season.

—*Jason F. Wright, novelist and pundit*

Life is a flame that is always burning itself out, but it catches fire again every time a child is born.
—*George Bernard Shaw, playwright and Nobel Laureate*

Children are love made visible.

—*American proverb*

A few days after we came home from the hospital, I sent a letter to a friend. . . . He responded, simply, "Everything is possible again." It was the perfect thing to write, because that was exactly how it felt. We could retell our stories and make them better, more representative or aspirational. Or we could choose to tell different stories. The world itself had another chance.

—Jonathan Safran Foer, novelist

Birth is the sudden opening of a window,
through which you look out upon a stupendous prospect.
For what has happened?
A miracle.
You have exchanged
nothing
for the possibility of
everything.
—William MacNeile Dixon, writer and professor

BECOMING

Here are the raw ingredients of motherhood: love, joy, and hope. Add a base—oneself before having children. Mix in instinct and hormones. Sprinkle in experience and expectation. We emerge from this crucible transformed. Pregnancy, it turns out, was only the beginning of self-expansion. In becoming mothers, we broaden our worldview, our circle of We. We become someone new. More startlingly, we realize that we're always in the process of becoming; as kids grow, we continue to change and adapt. To our surprise, we often like our new selves.

We delight in the beauty of the butterfly, but rarely admit the changes it has gone through to achieve that beauty.

—Maya Angelou, poet and novelist

Giving birth is little more than a set of muscular contractions granting passage of a child. Then the mother is born.

—Erma Bombeck, writer and humorist

The moment a child is born, the mother is also born. She never existed before. The woman existed, but the mother, never. A mother is something absolutely new.

—Osho, mystic and spiritual teacher

Motherhood is like Albania—you can't trust the descriptions in the books, you have to go there.

—Marni Jackson, journalist

Mighty is the force of motherhood. It transforms all things by its vital heat.

—George Eliot, novelist

Once, I was my mother's daughter. Now I am my daughter's mother.

—*Lisa Gardner, novelist*

Being a mother is who I am; it is a structure. No matter what happens to me or to my son in this life, I will be a mother. No one can change that or take it away.

—***Kim Gaines Eckert, psychologist***

Mother is a verb. It's something you do. Not just who you are.

—*Cheryl Lacey Donovan, writer, radio host, and religious leader*

Having a baby provided me with an entirely new set of eyes, ears, and unfortunately, breasts. It turned me into that most fierce, devoted, and visceral of creatures—a mother. It forced me to see and feel the despair and suffering of others from an entirely different construct. It allowed me to take notice of the aching grace and overwhelming beauty in the seemingly most inconsequential of life's moments.

—*Muffy Bolding, writer, actor, and feminist*

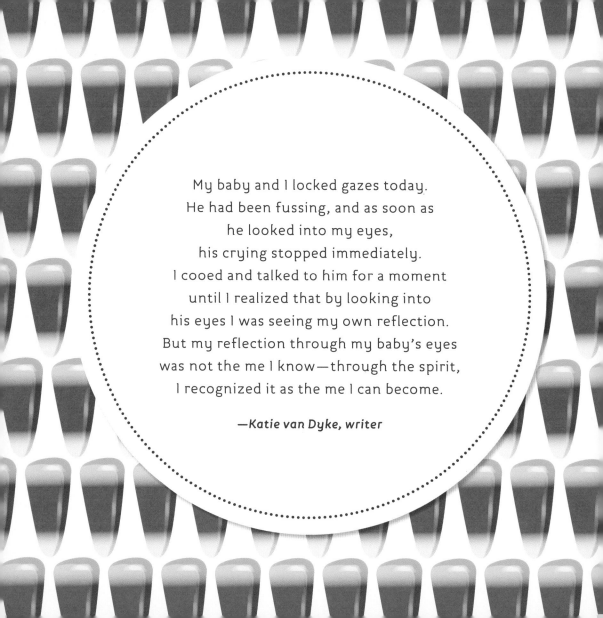

My baby and I locked gazes today.
He had been fussing, and as soon as
he looked into my eyes,
his crying stopped immediately.
I cooed and talked to him for a moment
until I realized that by looking into
his eyes I was seeing my own reflection.
But my reflection through my baby's eyes
was not the me I know—through the spirit,
I recognized it as the me I can become.

—*Katie van Dyke, writer*

You see yourself in them.

—Julie Walters, actor

Those helpless bundles of power and promise that come into our world show us our true selves—who we are, who we are not, who we wish we could be.

—Hillary Rodham Clinton, U.S. secretary of state

I am lying on my back on the floor, with [my daughter] Vanessa lying on my chest. She lifts her head and looks straight into my eyes for what seems like an eternity. I feel she is looking into my soul, that she knows me, that she is my conscience.

—Jane Fonda, actor and activist

I saw pure love when my son looked at me, and I knew that I had to make a good life for the two of us.

—Suzanne Somers, actor and singer

It was the tiniest thing I ever decided to put my whole life into.

—Terri Guillemets, anthologist

I was overcome with emotion on becoming a mother, and shocked at how quickly, and permanently, my worldview changed. I was stunned to find how territorial I felt, how flooded with love and fear for the baby's safety.

—*Rosanne Cash, singer-songwriter*

There is a tremendous amount of learning that takes place in the first year of your baby's life; the baby learns a lot, too.

—*Debra Gilbert Rosenberg , psychotherapist*

The important thing is this: To be able at any moment to sacrifice what we are for what we could become.

—*Charles Du Bos, critic*

I knew it was going to be the most extraordinary thing in my life, but how powerful it is, you can never know until you have a baby.

—*Céline Dion, singer-songwriter*

After your baby gets here, the dog will just be a dog.

—*Jodi Picoult, novelist*

Every once in awhile I'd meet . . . [a] childless friend for a walk, and it was like taking a peacock out on a leash. Look at her! I'd think. The childless friend would talk about her trip to Vietnam or Zihuatanejo and who said what to whom at which barbecue and her new interest in xeriscaping or Roller Derby, and as she talked I would just gaze. Secretly envious and secretly superior. I no longer had interests. I had a baby.

—*Claire Dederer, journalist*

Motherhood can become a true spiritual path: it requires one to constantly give up one's egocentric desires, to maintain constant awareness, and to be tuned in at all times to the needs of another being. As a mother you have to really see and feel what's going on.

—*Lama Tsultrim Allione, spiritual teacher*

There's a lot more to being a woman than being a mother, but there's a hell of a lot more to being a mother than most people suspect.

—*Roseanne Barr, actor and comedian*

You know you're a mother when the smallest whimper from your child can wake you from a dead sleep.

—Linda Poindexter, writer

For me, becoming a mom has brought to the surface a sensitivity the depth of which I never knew existed. It's hard to explain except to say that I feel more vulnerable and stripped of my personal defenses than ever before, and yet in some ways, I feel stronger. For me, becoming a mother also means that I feel happier than I could imagine and more sad than I thought possible. . . . Basically I am just being more alive and present in my own life than I can ever remember being.

—Brooke Shields, actor and model

Along with the joy of parenthood, with every child comes a piercing vulnerability. It is at once sublime and terrifying.

—David Sheff, journalist and memoirist

There really are places in the heart you don't even know exist until you love a child.

—Anne Lamott, writer

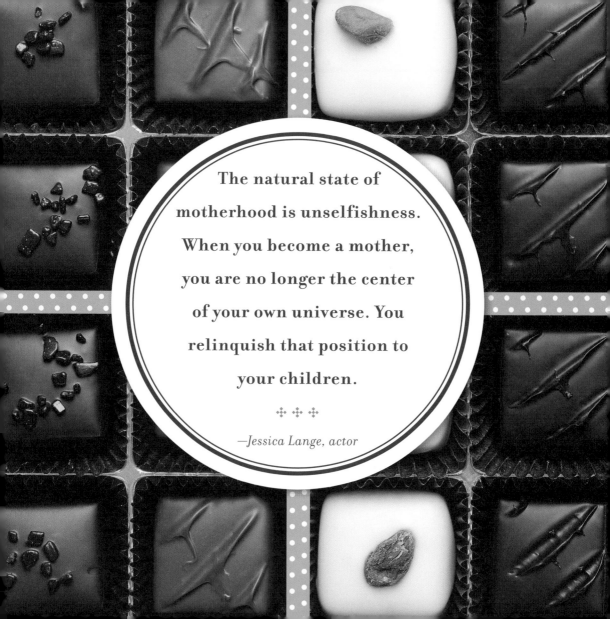

The natural state of motherhood is unselfishness. When you become a mother, you are no longer the center of your own universe. You relinquish that position to your children.

✤ ✤ ✤

—Jessica Lange, actor

Few things are sweeter than a new mom and her baby. Just a few days ago, I leaned over to peek at a total stranger's newborn in a stroller, and I looked back up at the mother and said, "Oh, how precious she is!" Tears welled in her eyes, and she couldn't even respond. I embraced this darling mom and said, "I so remember how easily the tears come after the birth of a child."

—Beth Moore and Dale McCleskey, writers

God sends children to enlarge our hearts
And make us unselfish
And full of kindly sympathies and affections.

—Mary Howitt, poet

That's the strange thing about being a mother: Until you have a baby, you don't even realize how much you were missing one.

—*Jodi Picoult, novelist*

Motherhood means holding a baby in your arms and accepting an existential truth: nothing, not one thing, not me with all my wonders and complexities, matters more than this.

—**Andrea Richesin, *writer and editor***

When you are a mother, you are never really alone in your thoughts. A mother always has to think twice: once for herself and once for her child.

—*Sophia Loren, actor*

Oddly, I've become calmer since having kids. You can't be absorbed with your own troubles when you're a mum—you just don't have time.

—**Kate Winslet, *actor***

I was so focused on things that didn't matter at the end of the day. Now I have what I do for a living in perspective. Working was everything to me, my entire identity, and once I got to step away from it, everything changed.

—*Jessica Alba, actor*

I used to grab the microphone and say, "...Let's get drunk tonight!" but I couldn't say that anymore. So at this party I was like, "Momma got out of the house tonight; let's celebrate!" I'm still the same person at heart, and I'll always be myself, but that night I saw myself growing up and having responsibilities that I'd never had before, and I liked it.

—*Kendra Wilkinson, television personality*

I remember people saying, "Believe me, everything in your life is going to change . . ." And I thought, "Why? That's such a bourgeois way of thinking." And then you have a child and yes, everything changes. It affects the way we live, what we do and where we go—everything. And I wouldn't have it any other way.

—*Maggie Gyllenhaal, actor*

Motherhood is an especially powerful experience because it involves learning under high-stakes conditions, which is just the sort of learning that drives change in the brain.

—*Michael Merzenich, neuroscientist*

And she, the new mother of a daughter, felt a fierceness come over her that seized at her heart, that made her feel as if her bones were turned to steel, as if she could turn herself into a weapon to keep this daughter of hers from having to be hurt by the world outside the ring of her arms.

—Lauren Groff, novelist

Noone told me I would feel like a wild animal ready to kill or be killed at a moment's notice with no hesitation at all right now for my baby. I would sit on the bed at night nursing Lally and I would imagine a lion jumping through the window. I would plan how to kill him. I knew the lion would be immediately dead. I knew that no matter what, my baby would survive.

—Peggy O'Mara, editor and publisher

The tigress does not bite when you tell her that her young are beautiful.

—Korean proverb

I'm becoming much more squishy and vulnerable and emotional.

—Kate Winslet, actor

Everything has a deeper meaning now.

—Holly Marie Combs, actor

It is not until you become a mother that your judgment slowly turns to compassion and understanding.

—Erma Bombeck, writer and humorist

When a baby is born the mother in particular enters into a new larger relationship with the world. She has become connected to all people. She is part of keeping us on earth—not the "us" comprised of individuals but the species itself. By protecting this one baby, this gift, a mother accepts life's clearest responsibility.

—*Gavin de Becker, writer and psychologist*

Before I'd hear about children who were hurt by poverty or violence, and I'd feel deeply for their mothers. But now, it's almost as if I'm personally wounded by their pain. I tell their stories with greater empathy now that I'm a mother, too.

—*Ann Curry, television news journalist*

Once you have a kid, you're like, "Oh yeah, if I'm exhausted because my kid was up all night with a cold, so are ten other people." It makes you more of a sympathetic human being.

—*Tina Fey, actor and comedian*

If there is anything that motherhood has taught me, it is that I am not just a mother to my two children, but to every child that I encounter. They all share the same innocence and vulnerability, and they are all precious and hold the promise of an enormous potential.

—Rania Al Abdullah, queen consort of Jordan

Becoming a mother makes you the mother of all children. From now on each wounded, abandoned, frightened child is yours. You live in the suffering mothers of every race and creed and weep with them. You long to comfort all who are desolate.

—Charlotte Gray, writer and historian

In becoming a mother I felt myself viscerally linked to all humanity and all of human history. . . . Caught in the powerful undertow that is generation, I felt the elemental currents and cross-currents of time, the layering of natural and human cycles.

—Robyn Sarah, poet

[Motherhood] sort of puts things into perspective, and it's about real life, and life is about people, what we give, what we take, what we share.

—*Halle Berry, actor*

Pregnancy doubled her, birth halved her, and motherhood turned her into Everywoman.

—*Erica Jong, novelist*

Being a mother means looking at every person with new eyes—because each of them was some mother's baby. Someone knew each hair, each tiny wrinkle, each fold behind a little ear.

—*Linda Aaker, lawyer and writer*

Kissing, hugging, laughing, cuddling, counseling, roughhousing—every loving thing we do is glue. Life pulls us in all directions, but if the bond we have with our kids is strong, all is fundamentally well. Of all attachments that kids make over the years—to plush animals, bits of cloth, bottle caps, and buzzing, babbling gadgets—moms are the ultimate and indispensable one. And when the bond weakens and gets brittle, as it surely does at times, just think of all the sweet times. Sugar, it turns out, is sticky.

Even when freshly washed and relieved of all obvious confections, children tend to be sticky.

—*Fran Lebowitz, writer and critic*

Attachment—the invisible threads that connect us to our children—woven from elements no lab could ever replicate: Love, Time, Connection, Closeness, Understanding . . . to name just a few.

—*Milli Hill, writer*

I wondered how long it took for a baby to become yours, for familiarity to set in. Maybe as long as it took a new car to lose that scent, or a brand-new house to gather dust. Maybe that was the process more commonly described as bonding: the act of learning your child as well as you know yourself.

—*Jodi Picoult, novelist*

The truth is, bonding occurs over time and there is no deadline.

—*Benjamin Spock, pediatrician*

Attachment is a process, not a finite event—repeat this mantra when perfection feels like it's slipping through your fingers.
—*Jessica Zucker, doctor and clinical psychologist*

Then someone placed her in my arms. She looked up at me. The crying stopped. Her eyes melted through me, forging a connection in me with their soft heat.
—*Shirley MacLaine, actor and activist*

Any human face is a claim on you, because you can't help but understand the singularity of it, the courage and loneliness of it. But this is truest of the face of an infant.
—*Marilynne Robinson, novelist*

Probably there is nothing in human nature more resonant with charges than the flow of energy between two biologically alike bodies, one of which has lain in amniotic bliss inside the other, one of which has labored to give birth to the other.

—*Adrienne Rich, poet and essayist*

Having a baby's sweet face so close to your own, for so long a time as it takes to nurse 'em, is a great tonic for a sad soul.

—*Erica Eisdorfer, novelist*

Babies love fat.

—*Kathryn Stockett, novelist*

Mother is physically intimate with her baby, obsessively kissing it, rocking it, caressing it. A soft, fragrant reservoir of love, her breast seems but an extension of the baby's body. The baby seems to be attached to her by the umbilical of its need. Loving mother is really a form of self-love. Beginning as one loving whole. A single world, mother and child, will in time become separate beings; just as lovers, becoming two separate beings, in time become one world, one whole.

—*Diane Ackerman, writer and naturalist*

Did you know babies are nauseated by the smell of a clean shirt?

—*Jeff Foxworthy, comedian*

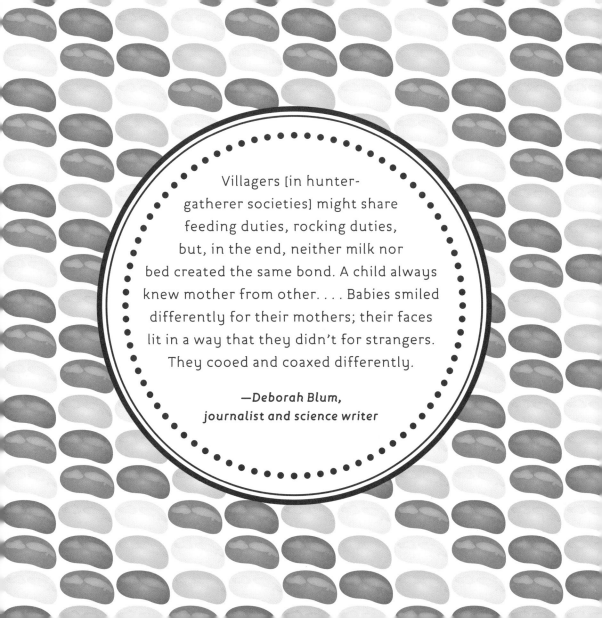

Villagers [in hunter-gatherer societies] might share feeding duties, rocking duties, but, in the end, neither milk nor bed created the same bond. A child always knew mother from other. . . . Babies smiled differently for their mothers; their faces lit in a way that they didn't for strangers. They cooed and coaxed differently.

—*Deborah Blum,*
journalist and science writer

Mothers and their children are in a category all their own. There's no bond so strong in the entire world. No love so instantaneous and forgiving.

—*Gail Tsukiyama, novelist*

She never quite leaves her children at home, even when she doesn't take them along.

—*Margaret Culkin Banning, novelist and activist*

What feeling is so nice as a child's hand in yours? So small, so soft and warm, like a kitten huddling in the shelter of your clasp.

—*Marjorie Holmes, writer*

When you're pregnant, you can think of nothing but having your own body to yourself again; yet after giving birth you realize that the biggest part of you is now somehow external, subject to all sorts of dangers and disappearance, so you spend the rest of your life trying to figure out how to keep her close enough for comfort.

—*Jodi Picoult, novelist*

Brain scans show synchrony between the brains of mother and child; but what they can't show is the internal bond that belongs to neither alone, a fusion in which the self feels so permeable it doesn't matter whose body is whose.

—*Diane Ackerman, writer and naturalist*

A rose can say "I love you,"
orchids can enthrall,
but a weed bouquet in a chubby fist,
yes, that says it all.
—Anonymous

When my son was two, he asked,
"Know how much I love you?"
"How much?" I responded.
"Two hundred and thirty-three!" was his answer.
"Why two hundred and thirty-three?"
"Well, isn't that the most there is?"

—*Ward Schumaker, illustrator*

She discovered with
great delight that one does not
love one's children just because
they are one's children
but because of the friendship
formed while raising them.

—*Gabriel García Márquez, novelist*

The mother's image is the first that stamps itself on the unwritten page of the young child's mind. It is her caress that first awakens a sense of security; her kiss, the first realization of affection; her sympathy and tenderness, the first assurance that there is love in the world.

—*David O. McKay, spiritual teacher*

Affection is responsible for nine-tenths of whatever solid and durable happiness there is in our lives.

—*C. S. Lewis, novelist, scholar, and poet*

The life of a mother is the life of a child: you are two blossoms on a single branch.

—*Karen Maezen Miller, writer and spiritual teacher*

My mother is me and I am she and we're all together.

—*Erica Jong, novelist*

You and your tenderness! Now you are mine
From your feet to your hair so golden and fine,
And your crumpled finger-tips . . . mine completely,
Wholly and sweetly;
Mine with kisses deep to smother,
No one so near to you now as your mother!
Others may hear your words of beauty,
But your precious silence is mine alone;
Here in my arms I have enrolled you,
Away from the grasping world I fold you,
Flesh of my flesh and bone of my bone!
—Lucy Maud Montgomery, poet and novelist, from "The Mother"

The tie which links mother and child is of such pure and immaculate strength as to be never violated.
—Washington Irving, writer and historian

You will always be your child's favorite toy.
—Vicki Lansky, writer and parenting expert

The invisible bond that gives the baby rein to discover his place in the world also brings the creeping baby back to home base. . . . In this way he recharges himself. He refuels on the loving energies that flow to him from his mother. Then he's off for another foray of adventure and exploration.

—*Louise J. Kaplan, psychoanalyst and scholar*

Give the choice between a mother's touch and food, baby monkeys will invariably choose the touch over food.

—*Jerry Ainsworth, writer and professor*

Once attachment is securely accomplished, children, like baby monkeys, are more likely to explore their environment, reflect curiosity, be persistent in complex tasks, be less fearful of change, and show less frustration when solving problems.

—*Robin Karr-Morse, family therapist*

You really don't understand human nature unless you know why a child on a merry-go-round will wave at his parents every time around—and why his parents will always wave back.

—*William D. Tammeus, writer*

You can never tell them [I love you] too many times, let them roll their eyes. . . . Life can sometimes be, for all of us, a bully and you need to have money in the bank. . . . Every time you say "I love you," you're putting money in the bank. You're not always going to be there to put money in the bank so I say you got to stock up so it will last a long time.

—*Ann Curry, television news journalist*

No matter what has happened or has been said, you still love your parent no matter what, and the parent loves the child no matter what.

—*Tori Spelling, actor*

One night, long after I put [my son] Gareth to bed, I heard him calling, "Ma-ma . . . Ma-ma . . . ," in a sweet singsong voice. When I opened his door he was lying in his Captain Hook bed, patting the space next to him. "Come be with me," he said. I lay down next to him, and he put his arm around me. "Please stay," he said. "For a long while."

"Forever," I told him.

—*Carey Goldberg, journalist*

[My daughter and I] play together like two children, laughing as though we have not a care in the world.

—*Eartha Kitt, singer and actor*

You may have tangible wealth untold;
Caskets of jewels and coffers of gold.
Richer than I you can never be
I had a mother who read to me.
—**Strickland Gillilan, poet and humorist,**
from "The Reading Mother"

Stories first heard at a mother's knee are never wholly forgotten—a little spring that never quite dries up in the journey through scorching years.

—*Paolo Ruffini, mathematician and philosopher*

Romance fails us and so do friendships, but the relationship of parent and child, less noisy than all the others, remains indelible and indestructible, the strongest relationship on earth.

—*Theodor Reik, psychoanalyst*

Children and mothers never truly part—
Bound in the beating of each other's heart.

—*Charlotte Gray, writer and historian*

What greater thing is there
for human souls than to feel
that they are joined for life—
to be with each other in silent
unspeakable memories.

✤ ✤ ✤

—*George Eliot, novelist*

Oh, what a loveliness her eyes
Gather in that one moment's space,
While peeping round the post she spies
Her darling's laughing face!
Oh, mother's love is glorifying,
On the cheek like sunset lying; In the eyes a
moisten'd light,
Softer than the moon at night!
—Edmund Clarence Stedman, poet

Once the realization is accepted that even between
the closest human beings infinite distances continue
to exist, a wonderful living side by side can grow up, if
they succeed in loving the distance between them which
makes it possible for each to see the other whole against
the sky.

—*Rainer Maria Rilke, poet*

Why does a mother love her newborn? Because the baby is hers? Even more. Because the baby is her. Her blood, her flesh. Her sinew and spine. Her hope. Her legacy.

—*Max Lucado, minister*

As children grow, they learn to apply the positive traits of bonding—trust, love, and care—to themselves. Adult relationships are related to people's ability to feel safe in the Universe, to believe in the essential goodness of others, and to care for themselves.

—*Charlotte Kasi, clinical counselor*

Smiles, giggles, snuggles, nuzzles. We crave the sweet stuff. It's addictive! Even when motherhood isn't so rewarding, we're hooked because there's always the prospect of more. Smelling, touching, hearing, seeing . . . children are a sensory delight. Who among us hasn't dug her nose in the crease of her child's neck and closed her eyes for a moment? Eye to eye, skin to skin, heart to heart. A child is a feast for the senses, and we never seem to get our fill of their wind-and-milk scented hair, luminous complexions, and gripping hugs. This addiction, it starts out as something physical—and along the way it becomes almost spiritual.

I don't know why they say, "you have a baby."
The baby has you.

—*Leo Gallagher, comedian*

This surprise is motherhood's great joy and darkest secret: Suddenly, you can't stop thinking about your child. You don't even stop when you're doing something important. . . . All that happens is a little dimmer switch inside you turns down a little, enough for you to concentrate on something else. But it never goes out completely.

—*Danielle Crittenden, journalist*

[Motherhood] is the one time when you can get enough of what you can never get enough of in the whole rest of life—the holding, kissing, the nuzzling and the stroking. Not only that, you can get it in public. It's officially sanctioned.

—*Christina Day, writer*

No one had told her what it would be like, the way she loved her children. What a thing of the body it was, as physically rooted as sexual desire but without its edge of danger. . . . Once the children were in the house, the air became more vivid and more heated: every object in the house grew more alive.

—Mary Gordon, writer and professor

The love of a baby involves not just the love of the idea of the baby, but the love of its body. Those tiny fingers and toes! The luscious smell of its little soft neck. The absurd superiority of one's own delicious baby over everyone else's baby.

—Elizabeth Berger, physician

The sweetest flowers in all the world—a baby's hands.

—Algernon Charles Swinburne, poet

He caught her child's smell; it was like the smell of day-old bread.

—John Banville, novelist

She smelled so sweet—
that delicious baby smell of warm clean skin
and the soap they use. That sweet smell
lingering around their mouths from drinking
only warm milk. That lovely cleaned smell
of new-laundered cotton and newly washed
best wool. Her coos of pleasure started again,
resonant by my ear, and when I turned my
face to sniff the warm little crease of her
plump neck she made me laugh aloud by
suddenly fixing her mouth onto my jaw line,
like a little vampire, and sucking noisily and
with evident satisfaction.

—*Philippa Gregory, novelist*

Cradling a swaddled infant in their arms, mothers would distractedly touch their lips to their babies' foreheads. Passing their toddlers in a hall, mothers would tousle their hair, even sweep them up in their arms and kiss them hard along their chins and necks until the children squealed with glee. Where else in life . . . could a woman love so openly and with such abandon?

—*Eowyn Ivey, novelist and reporter*

I understood once I held a baby in my arms, why some people have the need to keep having them.

—*Spalding Gray, actor, writer, and performance artist*

Place your baby on the carpet, face up, then crawl around on all fours, and announce, "I'm so hungry! I could eat a baby!" Then crawl over and gobble up the baby, starting at the feet, and periodically raising your head and shouting, "Great baby! Delicious!" Babies love this game.

—*Dave Barry, columnist and humorist*

Little Rose was indeed a delicious baby, all dimples and good humor and violet powder, with a skin as soft as a lily's leaf, and a happy capacity for allowing herself to be patted and cuddled without remonstrance.

—*Susan Coolidge, novelist*

I remember the smell of his baby-soft skin: warm milk, baby powder, and soap. Later, when he was big enough to dig in the flowerbeds and play on the swings, he smelled of dirt and dust and a child's sweet perspiration.

—*Christine O'Keefe Lafser, writer*

The smell of my son is as the smell of a field that the Lord has blessed.

—*Genesis 27:27*

A mother's body remembers her babies—the folds of soft flesh, the softly furred scalp against her nose. Each child has its own entreaties to body and soul.

—*Barbara Kingsolver, novelist and poet*

Sometimes when you pick up your child you can feel the map of your own bones beneath your hands, or smell the scent of your skin in the nape of his neck. This is the most extraordinary thing about motherhood—finding a piece of yourself separate and apart that all the same you could not live without.

—Jodi Picoult, novelist

There was a spot on the back of the neck, when the smell of fresh human life was exquisite. It smelled wholesome, warm, faintly sweet. Slightly earthy, yet pure and heavenly at the same time. . . . You picked your baby up and drew deeply through your nostrils, again and again over months and year, before finally exhaling in utter satisfaction.

—Debra Adelaide, novelist and educator

Parent and child may become bonded prenatally, through an exchange of odors or odor-like molecules.

—*Natalie Angier, science journalist*

Besides, they always smell of bread and butter.

—*George Gordon, Lord Byron, poet*

When a baby comes you can smell two things: the smell of flesh, which smells like chicken soup, and the smell of lilies, the flower of another garden, the spiritual garden.

—*Carlos Santana, musician*

I had always assumed kissing was a learned thing, like waving bye-bye or speaking a language. But since Maxie, I'd decided that it was innate, the adult version of something we know to do from the moment we're born. All of it tied together in the cycle of life.

—*Katherine Center, novelist*

What exactly does one's child smell like, there at the level of her still-forming flesh, below the creams and powder, below the fresh wind-dried diaper smell? Bread, maybe—warm bread. The yeasty scent of breast milk on her tongue. The fur of the nape of a kitten's neck. Adam or Eve before the fall.

—*Joyce Himnefield, novelist*

There are so many smells that come with a baby and I enjoy them all—even the stinky ones—because [my son] is just so delicious. Oh my God, that morning baby breath when they wake up and yawn? I love that smell.

—*Gwen Stefani, singer-songwriter and fashion designer*

[Babies'] joints are melted rubber, and even when you kiss them hard, in the passion of loving their existence, your lips sink down and seem never to find bone. Holding them against you, they melt and mold, as though they might at any moment flow back into your body.

—*Diana Gabaldon, novelist and ecologist*

My world shrunk to the size of her body. Immersed in her smell, her feedings, her needs, I couldn't imagine doing anything without her, that didn't involve her. . . . Totally absorbed, I lost myself within the tiny coil, the perfect comma, of her body.

—*Nora Okja Keller, novelist*

When a baby first looks at you...when it laughs that deep, unselfconscious gurgle; or when it cries and you pick it up and it clings sobbing to you...then you are—happy is not the precise word—filled.

— *Marilyn French, writer and feminist scholar*

The moment you have in your heart this extraordinary thing called love and feel the depth, the delight, the ecstasy of it, you will discover that for you the world is transformed.

—Jiddu Krishnamurti, philosopher

[My son] Dev squints up with dark blue eyes as if trying to make us out through smoke, and from the instant his gaze brushes by me, some inner light beams flip on. Never have I felt such blazing focus for another living creature. I can't stop looking at him. Joy, it is, which I've never known before, only pleasure or excitement. Joy is a different thing, because its focus exists outside the self—delight in something external, not satisfaction of some internal craving.

— Mary Karr, poet, essayist, and memoirist

Could a greater miracle take place than for us to look through each other's eyes for an instant?

—Henry David Thoreau, poet and essayist

The sun was starting to color the sky,
but the moon shone as though it were midnight.
I raised my daughter up into the darkness
and the colors. The baby fuzz on her hair was
lifted by the wind.
She tilted her head toward the sky,
opened her mouth and
gave me a gigantic gummy grin.
Oh how dull was the world before
there was a Mary.

—*Elizabeth Soutter Schwarzer, writer*

My baby's eyes! What light they hold;
What wonderful hints of wealth untold;
Of lands where the flowers never die,
Of tropic lands where the sunbeams lie,
On diamond fields and hills of gold
—Edith Willis Linn, poet, from "Baby's Eyes"

One unexpected bonus of motherhood is the visual beauty. I am enchanted by the sights of my children, the tones of skin, the clear eyes, the grace, the curve of a hand and cheek, to see them racing across the back lawn in a certain slant of light.

—*Jaroldeen Edwards, writer and public speaker*

As mothers, our one and only-ness is next to godliness. Are we not irreplaceable, inimitable, central, and core? Our love for our children, and theirs for us, is unlike that of any other. A mother's love is intimate, singular, and precious. Our say-so is unrivaled. We can heal a young person's wound with a kiss, embolden with a smile, read a mind at a glance, and make everything better. We inspire confidence. We represent the unconditional, the indubitable, the unlimited, the indispensable. In a child's early years, we are the world. As time passes, we merely become part of it. But we're always the first and true home.

Motherhood: All love begins and ends there.

—*Robert Browning, poet*

Her children rise up and bless her.

—*Proverbs 31:28*

Biology is the least of what makes someone a mother.

—*Oprah Winfrey, talk show host, actor, and philanthropist*

Most of all the other beautiful things in life come by twos and threes by dozens and hundreds. Plenty of roses, stars, sunsets, rainbows, brothers, and sisters, aunts and cousins, but only one mother in the whole world.

—*Kate Douglas Wiggin, educator and novelist*

There are thousands of women but only one mother.

—*Bolivian proverb*

God could not be everywhere, and therefore He made mothers.

—*Jewish proverb*

In a child's eyes, a mother is a goddess. She can be glorious or terrible, benevolent or filled with wrath, but she commands love either way. I am convinced that this is the greatest power in the universe.

—N. K. Jemisin, science fiction writer

A mother is a mother still, the holiest thing alive.

—Samuel Taylor Coleridge, poet

Mother is the name for God in the lips and hearts of little children.

—William Makepeace Thackeray, novelist

A little girl, when asked where her home was, replied, "where mother is."

—Keith L. Brooks, religious leader

You're the only thing they have.

—Heidi Klum, model and fashion designer

Whenever I came into the room, she'd light up, so happy to see me. No one ever in the course of my entire life was ever as happy to see me as she was. Looking back, now, I realize that you only ever need one person who lights up that way when you enter a room.

—*Adriana Trigiani, novelist, producer, and director*

To the world you may be just one person, but to one person you may be the world.

—*Brandi Snyder, writer*

Mother—that was the bank where we deposited all our hurts and worries.

—*T. DeWitt Talmage, minister*

There is no velvet so soft as a mother's lap, no rose as lovely as her smile, no path so flowery as that imprinted with her footsteps.

—*Archibald Thompson, conductor and composer*

The mother is everything—
she is our consolation in
sorrow, our hope in misery,
and our strength in weakness.
She is the source of love, mercy,
sympathy, and forgiveness.

✢ ✢ ✢

—Kahlil Gibran, *artist and poet*

Breast-feeding may succumb to the bottle; cuddling, fondling, and pediatric visits may also be done by fathers (and surely we could make life easier for mothers than we do), but when a child needs a mother to talk to, nobody else but a mother will do. A mother is a mother is a mother, as Gertrude Stein sure would have said had she become one.

—*Erica Jong, novelist*

A mother's arms are more comforting than anyone else's.

—*Diana, Princess of Wales*

No one worries about you like your mother. . . . There is no one on earth who knew you from the day you were born; who knew why you cried, or when you'd had enough food; who knew exactly what to say when you were hurting; and who encouraged you to grow a good heart.

—*Adriana Trigiani, novelist, producer, and director*

I'm your mother. I see all. Hear all. Know all.

—*Maria Snyder, novelist*

I don't know what it is about food your mother makes for you, especially when it's something that anyone can make—pancakes, meat loaf, tuna salad—but it carries a certain taste of memory.

—*Mitch Albom, writer, journalist, and broadcaster*

There is nothing in the world of art like the songs mother used to sing.

—*Billy Sunday, athlete*

There is none,
In all this cold and hollow world, no fount
Of deep, strong, deathless love, save that within
A mother's heart.
—*Felicia Hemans, poet*

No one in the world can take the place of your mother. Right or wrong, from her viewpoint you are always right. She may scold you for little things, but never for the big ones.

—*Harry Truman, U.S. president*

A mother is she who can take the place of all others.

—*Gaspard Mermillod, cardinal*

When God thought of mother, he must have laughed with satisfaction, and framed it quickly—so rich, so divine, so full of soul, power, and beauty was the conception.

—*Henry Ward Beecher, clergyman and social reformer*

A mother is a person who if she is not there when you get home from school you wouldn't know how to get your dinner, and you wouldn't feel like eating it anyway.

—**Anonymous**

What do girls do who haven't any mothers to help them through their troubles?

—**Louisa May Alcott, novelist**

Mother is the one we count on for the things that matter most of all.

—*Katharine Butler Hathaway, novelist*

Everybody knows that a good mother gives her children a feeling of trust and stability. She is their earth. She is the one they can count on for the things that matter most of all. She is their food and their bed and the extra blanket when it grows cold in the night; she is their warmth and their health and their shelter; she is the one they want to be near when they cry. She is the only person in the whole world in a whole lifetime who can be these things to her children. There is no substitute for her. Somehow even her clothes feel different to her children's hands from anybody else's clothes. Only to touch her skirt or her sleeve makes a troubled child feel better.

—*Katharine Butler Hathaway, novelist*

A child's hand in yours—what tenderness it arouses, what power it conjures. You are instantly the very touchstone of wisdom and strength.

—*Marjorie Holmes, writer*

There are many fathers, but only one mother.

—*Papiamentu proverb*

[My mother] was the force around which our world turned. . . .
One kiss could restore us to princedom. Without her, our lives
would dissolve into chaos.

—*Nicole Krauss, novelist*

One of the oldest human needs is having someone to wonder
where·you are when you don't come home at night.

—*Margaret Mead, anthropologist*

Mothers can forgive anything! Tell me all, and be sure that I will
never let you go, though the whole world should turn from you.

—*Louisa May Alcott, novelist*

Who is it that loves me and will love me forever with an
affection which no chance, no misery, no crime of mine
can do away? It is you, my mother.

—*Thomas Carlyle, writer, essayist, and historian*

I am your mother, the first mile of your road.

—*Kelly Corrigan, novelist*

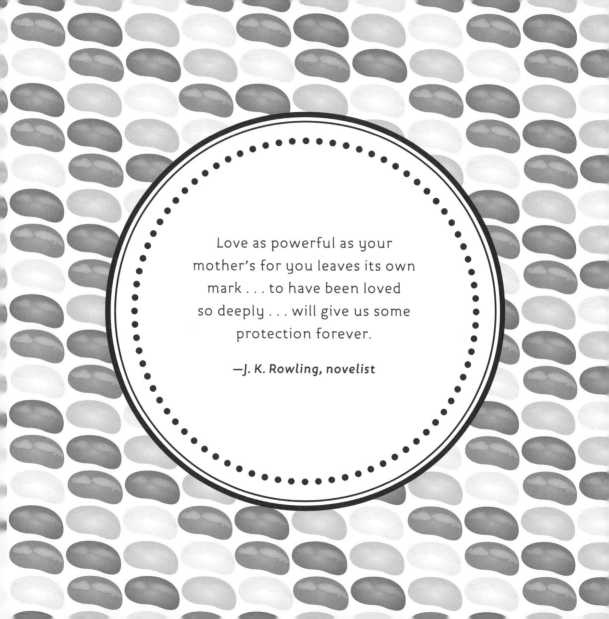

Love as powerful as your
mother's for you leaves its own
mark . . . to have been loved
so deeply . . . will give us some
protection forever.

—*J. K. Rowling, novelist*

If I were hanged on the highest hill,
Mother o' mine, O mother o' mine!
I know whose love would follow me still,
Mother o' mine, O mother o' mine!
—Rudyard Kipling, writer and poet, from "Mother o' Mine"

The love of husbands and wives may waver; brothers and sisters may become deep-rooted enemies; but a mother's love is so strong and unyielding that it usually endures all circumstances: good fortune and misfortune, prosperity and privation, honor and disgrace. A mother's love perceives no impossibilities.

—Anonymous

Mothers, I believe, intoxicate us. We idolize them and take them for granted. We hate them and blame them and exalt them more thoroughly than anyone else in our lives. We sift through the evidence of their love, reassure ourselves of their affection and its biological genesis. We can steal and lie and leave and they will love us.

—Megan Mayhew Bergman, writer

Nothing you become will disappoint me; I have no preconception that I'd like to see you be or do. I have no desire to foresee you, only to discover you. You can't disappoint me.

—*Mary Haskell, educator*

Being loved unconditionally by our mother does not necessarily mean that we are indulged or spoiled, that she never gets angry with us, or that she does not sometimes disapprove of what we do. A mother who loves her child unconditionally may draw boundaries, discipline, and indeed punish when she feels it is appropriate. But there is something deeper present, an enduring positive emotion that seems unaffected by transient disapproval.

—*Alyce Faye Cleese, psychotherapist*

To a child's ear, "mother" is magic in any language.

—*Arlene Benedict, writer*

Mama. I chose you.

—*Valya Dudycz Lupescu, novelist*

Whatever hurts the child, the father feels in his little finger, and the mother in her whole body.

—German proverb

One mother is worth more than ten fathers.

—Korean proverb

The father is the shoulder, the mother the soul.

—Tatar proverb

The real religion of the world comes from women much more than from men—from mothers most of all, who carry the key of our souls in their bosoms.

—Oliver Wendell Holmes Sr., physician, poet, and professor

Be a Mother who is committed to loving her children into standing on higher ground than the environment surrounding them. Mothers are endowed with a love that is unlike any other love on the face of the earth.

—**Marjorie Pay Hinckley, writer and spiritual teacher**

It had cost her to love, had cost her much to mother. It always does. But she would tell you that it's worth it, that there is no other way.

—*Stasi Eldredge, writer and religious leader*

There is in all this world
no fount of deep, strong, deathless love,
save that within a mother's heart.
—**Felicia Hemans, poet**

An ounce of mother is worth a ton of priest.

—**Spanish proverb**

Motherhood entitles us to reenter the enchanted garden of childhood. Here the world is new and vivid again. There's delight in every discovery! Mimic the birds, feed the squirrels, marvel at the surreal skin of frogs and butterflies. Imagine new worlds; give yourself goose bumps. What do the birds really do at night? Could we be characters in a story? There are no limits, no fixed lines between what's real and what's not. Embrace the incredible, marvel at the simple. Imagination and discovery are what childhood play is all about, and mothers get to go along for another ride. Miracles happen every minute.

Children make you want to start life over.

—*Muhammad Ali, boxer and activist*

Everything is ceremony in the wild garden of childhood.

—*Pablo Neruda, poet and politician*

Only where children gather is there any real chance of fun.

—*Mignon McLaughlin, journalist*

Tarry a moment to watch the chaos of a playground, Crayola-colored shirts of running children, all trying out their wings.

—*Dr. Sun Wolf, attorney and storyteller*

There are no seven wonders of the world in the eyes of a child. There are seven million.

—*Walt Streightiff, educator*

Deep meaning often lies in childish plays.

—*Friedrich Schiller, poet, philosopher, and historian*

Childhood is the world of miracle and wonder; as if creation rose, bathed in the light, out of the darkness, utterly new and fresh and astonishing.

—*Eugène Ionesco, playwright*

Mommies are just big little girls.

—*Anonymous*

There is a place in every childhood, an enchanted place where colors are brighter, the air softer, and the morning more fragrant than ever again.

—*Elizabeth Lawrence, writer*

At eight, he had once told his mother that he wanted to paint air.

—*Vladimir Nabokov, novelist*

What we remember from childhood we remember forever—permanent ghosts, stamped, inked, imprinted, eternally seen.

—*Cynthia Ozick, novelist and essayist*

What art can paint or gild
any object in afterlife with the glow which
Nature gives to the first baubles of childhood?
St. Peter's cannot have the magical power over us
that the red and gold covers of our first
picture book possessed.

—*Ralph Waldo Emerson, essayist and poet*

A three-year-old child is a being who gets almost
as much fun out of a fifty-six-dollar set of swings
as it does out of finding a small green worm.

—*Bill Vaughan, columnist*

Know what it is to be a child? It is to be something very different from the man of today. It is to have a spirit yet streaming from the waters of Baptism; it is to believe in belief; it is to be so little that elves can reach to whisper in your ear; it is to turn pumpkins into coaches, and mice into horses, lowness into loftiness, and nothing into everything, for each child had its fairy godmother in its soul.

—*Percy Bysshe Shelley, poet*

Children hallow small things. A child is a priest of the ordinary, fulfilling a sacred office that absolutely no one else can fill. The simplest gesture, the ephemeral movement, the commonest object all become precious beyond words when touched, noticed, lived by one's own dear child.

—*Mike Mason, writer*

Play is the highest form of research.

—*Albert Einstein, theoretical physicist*

Only a child sees things with perfect clarity, because it hasn't developed all those filters which prevent us from seeing things that we don't expect to see.

—Douglas Adams, writer and dramatist

Remember this, Mama, I tell myself as I watch my daughter examine each blueberry I've given her for a snack before she puts it in her mouth. They're just blueberries to me. To her, each one looks different. Each one tastes slightly different. . . . She sees a world I've forgotten exists.

—Kirstin Hendrickson, chemist and writer

The path of development is a journey of discovery that is clear only in retrospect, and it's rarely a straight line.

—Eileen Kennedy-Moore, writer and psychologist

Children find everything in nothing; men find nothing in everything.

—Giacomo Leopardi, poet and philosopher

Pausing to listen to an airplane in the sky, stooping to watch a ladybug on a plant, sitting on a rock to watch the waves crash over the quayside—children have their own agendas and timescales. As they find out more about their world and their place in it, they work hard not to let adults hurry them.

—*Cathy Nutbrown, educator*

Sweet childish days, that were as long
As twenty days are now.
—**William Wordsworth, poet, from "To a Butterfly"**

It is in playing, and only in playing, that the individual child or adult is able to be creative and to use the whole personality, and it is only in being creative that the individual discovers the self.

—**D. W. Winnicott, pediatrician and psychoanalyst**

Play is our brain's favorite way of learning.

—*Diane Ackerman, writer and naturalist*

To a toddler, even a simple walk around the block is a great adventure. My toddler doesn't walk with any destination in mind. She takes it one step at a time, and every step or so, there is something that must be investigated. A small stone, different from any she's seen before. A single crocus, poking through grey earth, barely noticeable to the adult eye. Grass growing up between sections of the sidewalk. She observes, hypothesizes, and experiments.

—*Alice Callahan, writer and research scientist*

A young child is, indeed, a true scientist, just one big question mark. What? Why? How? I never cease to marvel at the recurring miracle of growth, to be fascinated by the mystery and wonder of this brave enthusiasm.

—*Victoria Wagner, artist*

To show a child what once delighted you, to find the child's delight added to your own—this is happiness.

—*J. B. Priestley, novelist and playwright*

When you become a parent . . .
you become the person
controlling the bubble of
innocence around a child,
regulating it.

✥ ✥ ✥

—*Kazuo Ishiguro, novelist*

You are worried about seeing him spend his early years in doing nothing. What! Is it nothing to be happy? Nothing to skip, play, and run around all day long? Never in his life will he be so busy again.

—Jean-Jacques Rousseau, writer and philosopher

Kids: they dance before they learn there is anything that isn't music.

—William Stafford, poet and activist

We grown-up people think that we appreciate music, but if we realized the sense that an infant has brought with it of appreciating sound and rhythm, we would never boast of knowing music. The infant is music itself.

—Hazrat Inayat Khan, spiritual teacher

Every child is born a genius.

—Richard Buckminster Fuller, architect, inventor, and futurist

I've met more than my share of young prodigies—kids who were pushed to skip grades, memorize Latin names for every insect, and greet all adults with firm handshakes. They're weird, and not in a good way, like a corgi wearing a tuxedo: sure it's cute, but does it truly know joy?

—*Brett Berk, educator and consultant*

In play a child always behaves beyond his average age, above his daily behavior. In play it is as though he were a head taller than himself.

—*Lev Vygotsky, psychologist*

A child's existence is a bright, soft element of joy.

—*C. N. Douglas, poet*

If I had influence with the good fairy who is supposed to preside over the christening of all children I should ask that her gift to each child in the world be a sense of wonder so indestructible that it would last throughout life.

—*Rachel Carson, conservationist*

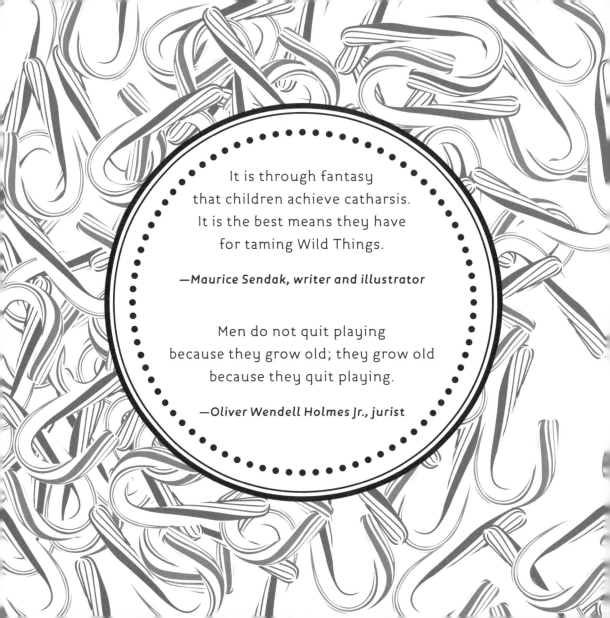

It is through fantasy
that children achieve catharsis.
It is the best means they have
for taming Wild Things.

—Maurice Sendak, writer and illustrator

Men do not quit playing
because they grow old; they grow old
because they quit playing.

—Oliver Wendell Holmes Jr., jurist

Only those who look with the eyes of children can lose themselves in the object of their wonder.

—*Eberhard Arnold, writer and philosopher*

Children are remarkable for their intelligence and ardour, for their curiosity, their intolerance of shams, the clarity and ruthlessness of their vision.

—*Aldous Huxley, novelist*

The plays of natural lively children are the infancy of art. Children live in a world of imagination and feeling. They invest the most insignificant object with any form they please, and see in it whatever they wish to see.

—*Adam Oehlenschläger, poet and playwright*

To have a childhood means to live a thousand lives before the one.

—*Rainer Maria Rilke, poet*

As astronauts and space travelers, children puzzle over the future; as dinosaurs and princesses they unearth the past. As weather reporters and restaurant workers they make sense of reality; as monsters and gremlins they make sense of the unreal.

—*Gretchen Owocki, educator*

Children see magic because they look for it.

—*Christopher Moore, novelist*

Your kid is your kid, and wherever they take you, you go.

—*Kelly Corrigan, novelist*

When I was younger I remember watching two drops of rain roll down a window and pretending it was a race.

—*Anonymous*

Because children grow up, we think a child's purpose is to grow up. But a child's purpose is to be a child.

—*Tom Stoppard, playwright*

The illusions of childhood are necessary experiences: a child should not be denied a balloon because an adult knows that sooner or later it will burst.

—Marcelene Cox, writer

Living in that childish wonder is a most beautiful feeling— I can so well remember it. There was always something more— behind and beyond everything— to me, the golden spectacles were very, very big.

—Kate Greenaway, illustrator

Is the world all grown up? Is childhood dead? Or is there not in the bosom of the wisest and the best some of the child's heart left, to respond to its earliest enchantments?

—Charles Lamb, poet and essayist

Deep meaning often lies in childish plays.

—Friedrich Schiller, poet, philosopher, and historian

I remember my childhood names
for grasses and secret flowers.
I remember where a toad may live and
what time the birds awaken in the summer
—and what trees and seasons smelled like—
how people looked and walked and smelled even.
The memory of odors is very rich.

—John Steinbeck, *novelist*

Childhood is measured out by sounds
and smells and sights,
before the dark hour of reason grows.

—John Betjeman, *poet and broadcaster*

The books of our childhood offer a vivid door to our own pasts, and not necessarily for the stories we read there, but for the memories of where we were and who we were when we were reading them; to remember a book is to remember the child who read that book.

—*Lewis Buzbee, memoirist and poet*

I remember I used to half believe and wholly play with fairies when I was a child. What heaven can be more real than to retain the spirit-world of childhood, tempered and balanced by knowledge and common sense?

—*Beatrix Potter, writer, illustrator, and natural scientist*

It's the sounds and smells of earlier years coming back to you. . . . It's the sky you used to look at when you were a child. You understand ideas again. Money has no power.

—*John LeCarré, novelist*

One thing I had learned from watching chimpanzees with their infants is that having a child should be fun.

—*Jane Goodall, anthropologist*

If a child is to keep his inborn sense of wonder . . . he needs the companionship of at least one adult who can share it, rediscovering with him the joy, excitement and mystery of the world we live in.

—*Rachel Carson, conservationist*

In every house a child that in mere play utters oracles, & knows not that they are such. 'Tis as easy as breath. 'Tis like this gravity, which holds the Universe together, & none knows what it is.

—*Ralph Waldo Emerson, essayist and poet*

No sweeter, holier sound to heaven can float
Than childhood's laughter, or the free bird's note
—*Guy de Maupassant, poet*

To the art of working well a civilized race would add the art of playing well.

—*George Santayana, philosopher*

That humanity which is revealed in all its intellectual splendor during the sweet and tender age of childhood should be respected with a kind of religious veneration. It is like the sun which appears at dawn or a flower just beginning to bloom.

—*Maria Montessori, educator*

Did you know that childhood is the only time in our lives when insanity is not only permitted to us but expected?

—*Louis de Bernières, novelist*

If we can slow ourselves down a bit from the hurried rush of Western life to go at our children's pace for a while, we might notice things we might otherwise miss. "Look, Mommy!" [my daughter] will exclaim, "This tulip is so pink!" and "Oh Mommy! I love wormies, they're soooo cute!" I remember how beautiful each flower, each sunset, each bug was to me when I was a child. When I can quiet my mind and look through my daughter's eyes, I am able to recapture some of the beauty and innocence of childhood.

—Cheryl Dimof, writer

To see a child touch the piano keys for the first time, to watch a small body slice through the surface of the water in a clean dive, is to experience the shock, not of the new, but of the familiar revisited as if it were strange and wonderful.

—*Anna Quindlen, journalist and novelist*

Memories of childhood were the dreams that stayed with you after you woke.

—*Julian Barnes, novelist*

Behavioral traits such as curiosity about the world, flexibility of response, and playfulness are common to practically all young mammals but are usually rapidly lost with the onset of maturity in all but humans. Humanity has advanced, when it has advanced, not because it has been sober, responsible and cautious, but because it has been playful, rebellious, and immature.

—*Tom Robbins, novelist*

O mother-my-love, if you'll give me your hand,
And go where I ask you to wander,
I will lead you away to a beautiful land,—
The Dreamland that's waiting out yonder.
We'll walk in a sweet posie-garden out there,
Where moonlight and starlight are streaming,
And the flowers and the birds are filling the air
With the fragrance and music of dreaming.
—Eugene Field, poet, from "Child and Mother"

Imagining yourself a child, it seems, can quite literally make your mind more flexible, more original, more open to creative input and more capable of generating creative output.

—Maria Konnikova, psychologist

HEART

Love is the molten core of motherhood. Love is fuel and the engine. Love is the salve and the magic. It's the currency, the commodity, and the investment. Loving our children binds us and broadens us, ties us and frees us. It's powerful and tender, blind and focused. It offers insight and intuition. A mother's love is unconditional and indispensable. It's the foundation, the structure, and the peak. Love is sure footing. Love is the meaning, the purpose, and the path. To mother is to love.

The only love that I really believe in is a mother's love for her children.

—*Karl Lagerfeld, fashion designer*

Asking me to describe my son is like asking me to hold the ocean in a paper cup.

—*Jodi Picoult, novelist*

Kindness to children, love for children, goodness to children — these are the only investments that never fail.

—*Henry David Thoreau, poet and essayist*

No one told me that the love I'd feel for my child would be so pervasive and consuming.

—*Amy Hatvany, novelist*

It's easy to complain about our children. But when we want to express our joy, our love, the words elude us. The feelings are almost so sacred they defy speech.

—*Joan McIntosh, educator*

God, she loved this kid. Wendy had one of those waves, the ones that sneak up on parents and crush them and make them just want to wrap their arms around their kid and never let him go.

—*Harlan Coben, novelist*

With every child, your heart grows bigger and stronger ... there is no limit to how much or how many people you can love, even though at times you feel as though you could burst—you don't—you just love even more.

—*Yasmin Le Bon, model*

"Sometimes," said Pooh, "the smallest things take up the most room in your heart."

—*A. A. Milne, writer and playwright*

Whatever else is unsure in this stinking dunghole of a world a mother's love is not.

—*James Joyce, novelist*

When you begin to touch your heart or let your heart be touched, you begin to discover that it's bottomless, that it doesn't have any resolution, that this heart is huge, vast, and limitless. You begin to discover how much warmth and gentleness is there, as well as how much space.

—*Pema Chodron, Buddhist nun and spiritual teacher*

Hast thou sounded the depths of yonder sea,
And counted the sands that under it be?
Hast thou measured the height of heaven above?
Then may'st thou mete out a mother's love.
—*Emily Taylor, poet, from "A Mother's Love"*

Mother's love is peace. It need not be acquired, it need not be deserved.

—*Erich Fromm, psychologist*

There is no division nor subtraction in the heart-arithmetic of a good mother. There are only addition and multiplication.

—*Bess Streeter Aldrich, writer*

I LOVE THESE LITTLE PEOPLE; AND IT IS NOT A SLIGHT THING WHEN THEY, WHO ARE SO FRESH FROM GOD, LOVE US.

—CHARLES DICKENS, NOVELIST

My mother said she loved me from when I was only an idea in her imagination. She loved me more when I was an egg in her womb. She loved me more when her egg was being fertilized, as she secretly lay in the tall grass surrounding her home, bursting with passion and writhing with pleasure. My mother said she loved me more every day that I became more than an idea, and that this intense love is what led her to do whatever it took to bring me into this world properly, to raise me well and keep me safe.

—Sister Souljah, artist and activist

A mother's love is like the tree of life.
Strong in spirit,
Peaceful, wise, and beautiful.
—American proverb

A mother is the only person on earth who can divide her love among ten children and each child still has all her love.

—Anonymous

A person don't got a soul until that person is loved. If a mother loves her baby—*wants* her baby—it's got a soul from the moment she knows it's there. The moment you're loved, that's when you got your soul.

—*Neal Shusterman, novelist*

What it's like to be a parent: It's one of the hardest things you'll ever do but in exchange it teaches you the meaning of unconditional love.

—*Nicholas Sparks, novelist*

Mom had the kind of love for her that you could feel, like it was part of the atmosphere.

—*Peter Abrahams, novelist*

The degree of loving is measured by the degree of giving.

—*Edwin Louis Cole, spiritual teacher*

The heart of a mother is a deep abyss at the bottom of which you will always find forgiveness.

—Honoré de Balzac, novelist and playwright

I go by instinct— I don't worry about experience.

—Barbra Streisand, singer-songwriter

A mother's love is patient and forgiving when all others are forsaking, and it never fails or falters, even though the heart is breaking.
—Helen Steiner Rice, poet

A mother's love endures through all; in good repute, in bad repute, in the face of the world's condemnation, a mother still loves on, and still hopes that her child may turn from his evil ways, and repent; still she remembers the infant smiles that once filled her bosom with rapture, the merry laugh, the joyful shout of his childhood, the opening promise of his youth; and she can never be brought to think him all unworthy.

—*Washington Irving, writer and historian*

Love—especially that of a child—was the most necessary weight you can endure in life, even if it hurts, even if it tugs bags under the skin of your eyes. Without it, the soul skitters to the edge of the world and teeters there, confused.

—*Tiffany Baker, novelist*

Some are kissing mothers and some are scolding mothers, but it is love just the same, and most mothers kiss and scold together.

—*Pearl S. Buck, novelist*

The mother loves her child most divinely, not when she surrounds him with comfort and anticipates his wants, but when she resolutely holds him to the highest standards and is content with nothing less than his best.

—*Hamilton Wright Mabie, essayist and critic*

The beetle saw its child on a wall and said, "a pearl on a thread."

—*Arabian proverb*

Mothers see the angel in us because the angel is there.

—*Booth Tarkington, novelist and dramatist*

A mother is the truest friend we have, when trials, heavy and sudden, fall upon us; when adversity takes the place of prosperity; when friends who rejoice with us in our sunshine, desert us when troubles thicken around us, still will she cling to us, and endeavor by her kind precepts and counsels to dissipate the clouds of darkness, and cause peace to return to our hearts.

—*Washington Irving, writer and historian*

A father may turn his back on his child, brothers and sisters may become inveterate enemies, husbands may desert their wives, wives their husbands. But a mother's love endures through all.

—*Washington Irving, writer and historian*

Before becoming a mother I had a hundred theories on how to bring up children. Now I have seven children and only one theory: love them, especially when they least deserve to be loved.

—*Kate Samperi, writer*

It's a funny thing about mothers and fathers. Even when their own child is the most disgusting little blister you could ever imagine, they still think that he or she is wonderful.

—*Roald Dahl, writer, poet, and pilot*

A mother's love for her child is like nothing else in the world. It knows no law, no pity. It dares all things and crushes down remorselessly all that stands in its path.

—*Agatha Christie, novelist*

A mother understands what a child does not say.

—*Jewish proverb*

Mother's intuition can tell you everything with kids. Mothers have a sixth sense. You're in tune with your child. You can hear them calling for help.

—*Jane Seymour, actor*

Most mothers are instinctive philosophers.

—*Harriet Beecher Stowe, author and activist*

Love takes up where knowledge leaves off.

—*Thomas Aquinas, priest*

Loving a child is a circular
business . . . the more you give,
the more you get, the more you
get, the more you give.

—*Penelope Leach, psychologist*

A mother knows what her child's gone through, even if she didn't see it herself.

—*Pramoedya Ananta Toer, novelist*

People always talked about a mother's uncanny ability to read her children, but that was nothing compared to how children could read their mothers.

—*Anne Tyler, novelist*

Are we not like two volumes of one book?

—*Marceline Desbordes-Valmore, poet*

You can fool some of the people all of the time, and all of the people some of the time, but you can't fool mom.

—*Captain Penny, children's television host*

You develop a third eye where you kind of know where they are in a room at all times.

—*Jodie Foster, actor*

Mother love—that divine gift which comforts, purifies, and strengthens all who seek it.

—Louisa May Alcott, novelist

[A mother] has known the child as part of herself, and even if the child is born and is growing the mother goes on feeling a subtle rhythm with the child. If the child feels ill, a thousand miles away the mother will immediately feel it. She may not be aware of what has happened but she will become depressed; she may not be aware that her child is suffering but she will start suffering. . . . The mother and the child always remain joined together with subtle energy, waves, because they go on vibrating on the same wavelength.

—Osho, mystic and spiritual teacher

To love at all is to be vulnerable. Love anything and your heart will be wrung and possibly broken. If you want to make sure of keeping it intact you must give it to no one, not even an animal. Wrap it carefully round with hobbies and little luxuries; avoid all entanglements. Lock it up safe in the casket or coffin of your selfishness. But in that casket, safe, dark, motionless, airless, it will change. It will not be broken; it will become unbreakable, impenetrable, irredeemable. To love is to be vulnerable.

—*C. S. Lewis, novelist, scholar, and poet*

One is a mother in order to understand the inexplicable. One is a mother to lighten the darkness. One is a mother to shield when lightning streaks the night, when thunder shakes the earth, when mud bogs one down. One is a mother in order to love without beginning or end.

—*Mariama Bâ, writer and feminist*

Motherhood: All love begins and ends there.

— *Robert Browning, poet*

Love is the condition
in which the happiness of
another person is essential
to your own.

✢ ✢ ✢

—Robert Heinlein, *novelist*

For every action there is a reaction. For better and for worse, it seems that nothing we moms do goes unobserved by our children. We are the mold, the model. In the early years of parenting, we set the tone and the tune. We're front and center stage. As time passes, we play supporting roles. We're cheerleaders, mentors, enforcers, and guides. We are the shoulders on which our children stand. We offer dreams, beliefs, values. Of course, influence goes both ways. It's a loop, not a line, and children have as much sway over us as we do over them. This loop goes on and on—it lasts a lifetime.

The child supplies the power but the parents have to do the steering.

—*Benjamin Spock, pediatrician*

Everything depends on upbringing.

—*Leo Tolstoy, novelist*

I plan to give you love, nurturing—and enough dysfunction to make you interesting.

—*Anonymous*

Children have never been very good at listening to adults but they have never failed to imitate them.

—*James Baldwin, novelist*

I believe that what a woman resents is not so much giving herself in pieces as giving herself purposelessly.

—*Anne Morrow Lindbergh, writer, poet, and aviator*

[Kids] don't remember what you try to teach them. They remember what you are.

—Jim Henson, writer and puppeteer

Children are what the mothers are.

—Walter Landor, writer and poet

I've learned that people will forget what you said, people will forget what you did, but people will never forget how you made them feel.

—Maya Angelou, poet and novelist

Live your life the way you want your kids to live theirs.

—Michael First, psychiatrist

Setting an example is not the main means of influencing another, it is the only means.

—Albert Einstein, theoretical physicist

A mother's children are portraits of herself.

—*Anonymous*

A mother who radiates self-love and self-acceptance actually vaccinates her daughter against low self-esteem.

—*Naomi Wolf, writer, political consultant, and activist*

Children are like wet cement. Whatever falls on them makes an impression.

—*Haim Ginott, psychologist and educator*

A mother has far greater influence on her children than anyone else, and she must realize that every word she speaks, every act, every response, her attitude, even her appearance and manner of dress affect the lives of her children and the whole family. It is while the child is in the home that he gains from his mother the attitudes, hopes, and beliefs that will determine the kind of life he will live and the contribution he will make to society.

—*N. Eldon Tanner, teacher and politician*

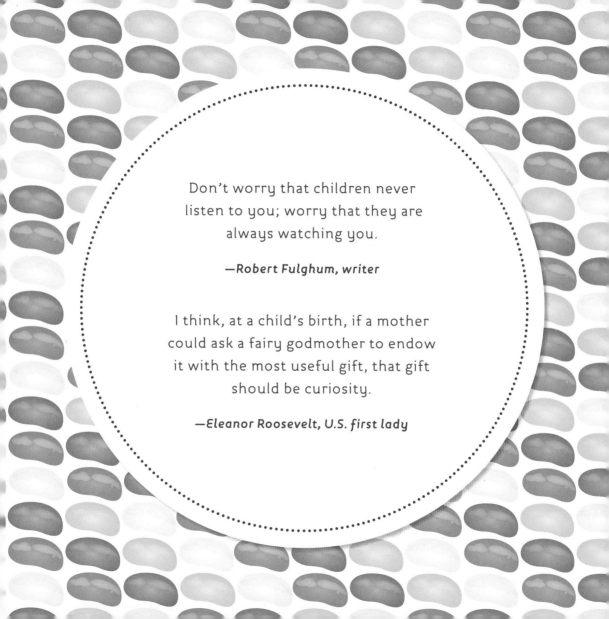

Don't worry that children never listen to you; worry that they are always watching you.

—*Robert Fulghum, writer*

I think, at a child's birth, if a mother could ask a fairy godmother to endow it with the most useful gift, that gift should be curiosity.

—*Eleanor Roosevelt, U.S. first lady*

Setting a good example for your children takes all the fun out of middle age.

—*William Feather, writer and publisher*

Yes, Mother. I can see you are flawed. You have not hidden it. That is your greatest gift to me.

—*Alice Walker, novelist*

Do not try to produce an ideal child, it would find no fitness in this world.

—*Herbert Spencer, philosopher, biologist, and political scientist*

To endure is the first thing that a child ought to learn, and that which he will have the most need to know.

—*Jean-Jacques Rousseau, writer and philosopher*

The art of mothering is to teach the art of living to children.

—*Elaine Heffner, writer*

If we don't shape our kids, they will be shaped by outside forces that don't care what shape our kids are in.

—*Louise Hart, writer and psychologist*

Bring up your children in safety, educate them, keep them healthy, teach them how to care for themselves and others, allow them to develop in their own way among adults who are sane and responsible, who know the value of the world and not its economic potential. It means art, it means time, it means all the invisibles never counted by the GDP and the census figures. It means knowing that life has an inside as well as an outside. And I think it means love.

—*Jeanette Winterson, novelist*

When you put faith, hope and love together, you can raise positive kids in a negative world.

—*Zig Ziglar, motivational speaker*

You cannot antagonize and influence at the same time.

—*J. S. Knox, writer*

If you want your children to improve, let them overhear the nice things you say about them to others.

—*Haim Ginott, psychologist and educator*

Affirming words from moms and dads are like light switches. Speak a word of affirmation at the right moment in a child's life and it's like lighting up a whole roomful of possibilities.

—*Gary Smalley, family counselor*

There was a child went forth every day;
And the first object he look'd upon, that object he
became;
And that object became part of him for the day, or a
certain part of the day, or for many
years, or
stretching cycles of years.

. . . . . .

His own parents,
He that had father'd him, and she that had conceiv'd him
in her womb, and
birth'd
him,
They gave this child more of themselves than that;
They gave him afterward every day—they became part of
him.
—Walt Whitman, poet,
from "There Was a Child Went Forth"

Children should be taught not the little virtues but the great ones. Not thrift but generosity and an indifference to money; not caution but courage and a contempt for danger; not a desire for success but a desire to be and to know.

—*Natalia Ginzburg, writer*

If we are to teach real peace in this world, and if we are to carry on a real war against war, we shall have to begin with the children.

—*Mohandas Gandhi, political and spiritual leader*

I dream of giving birth to a child who will ask, Mother, what was war?

—*Eve Merriam, poet and writer*

Praise your children openly, reprehend them secretly.

—*George W. Cecil, writer*

We should say to each of them: Do you know what you are?
You are a marvel. You are unique. In all the years that have
passed, there has never been another child like you. Your legs,
your arms, your clever fingers, the way you move.
You may become a Shakespeare, a Michelangelo, a Beethoven.
You have the capacity for anything. Yes, you are a marvel.

—Pablo Casals, cellist and conductor

Children must early learn the beauty of generosity. They are
taught to give what they prize most, that they may taste the
happiness of giving.

—Charles Alexander (Ohiyesa) Eastman, physician and writer

What you teach your own children is what you really
believe in.

— Cathy Warner Weatherford, writer

A child is not a vase to be filled but a fire to be lit.

—François Rabelais, doctor, monk, and scholar

Parents can plant magic in a child's mind through certain words spoken with some thrilling quality of voice, some uplift of the heart and spirit.

—Robert MacNeil, novelist and television news journalist

If you really want children to hear every word that you have to say, lean over them, put your lips close to their ears, and whisper to them. The complete privacy of the interaction and the heat of your breath in their ears will bring total attention to your every word.

—Tom Sturges, writer

The voice of parents is the voice of gods, for to their children they are heaven's lieutenants.

—William Shakespeare, playwright

What we want is to see the child in pursuit of knowledge, and not knowledge in pursuit of the child.

—*George Bernard Shaw, playwright and Nobel Laureate*

When I was 5 years old, my mother always told me that happiness was the key to life. When I went to school, they asked me what I wanted to be when I grew up. I wrote down "happy." They told me I didn't understand the assignment, and I told them they didn't understand life.

—*John Lennon, musician and singer-songwriter*

I just want my kids to love who they are, have happy lives and find something they want to do and make peace with that. Your job as a parent is to give your kids not only the instincts and talents to survive, but help them enjoy their lives.

—*Susan Sarandon, actor*

Children are living beings—more living than grown-up people who have built shells of habit around themselves. Therefore it is absolutely necessary for their mental health and development that they should not have mere schools for their lessons, but a world whose guiding spirit is personal love.

—*Rabindranath Tagore, poet, philosopher, and Nobel Laureate*

A mother is not a person to lean on but a person to make leaning unnecessary.

—*Dorothy Canfield Fisher, writer and social activist*

If you want children to keep their feet on the ground, put some responsibility on their shoulders.

—*Abigail Van Buren, advice columnist*

Tell me and I forget, teach me and I may remember, involve me and I learn.

—*Benjamin Franklin, U.S. founding father*

In the end, it's not what
we keep our children from
that will save them.
It's what we put into them
in the first place.

✦ ✦ ✦

—Marc Parent, writer

A wise parent humors the desire for independent action, so as to become the friend and advisor when his absolute rule shall cease.

—*Elizabeth Gaskell, novelist*

Tough and funny and a little bit kind: that is as near to perfection as a human being can be.

—*Mignon McLaughlin, journalist*

If from infancy you treat children as gods, they are liable in adulthood to act as devils.

—*P. D. James, novelist*

Govern a family as you would cook a small fish—very gently.

—*Chinese proverb*

As parents, we strive to raise kids certain of our love and confident of their next meal, which, let's face it, means giving up a little leverage.

—*Robert Brault, writer*

I have found the best way to give advice to your children is to find out what they want and then advise them to do it.

—*Harry S. Truman, U.S. president*

One thing I know for sure about raising children is that every single day a kid needs discipline. . . . But also every single day a kid needs a break.

—*Anne Lamott, writer*

Mothers have as powerful an influence over the welfare of future generations as all other earthly causes combined.

—*John S. C. Abbott, pastor*

What we want them to know five years from now has to be part of the conversation today.

—*Rosemary Wixom, religious leader*

Don't limit a child to your own learning, for he was born in another time.

—*Jewish proverb*

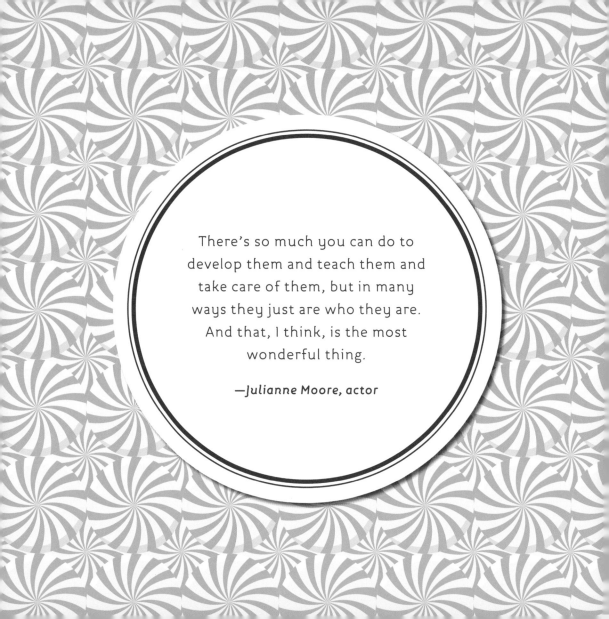

There's so much you can do to develop them and teach them and take care of them, but in many ways they just are who they are. And that, I think, is the most wonderful thing.

—Julianne Moore, actor

Influence: What you think you have until you try to use it.
—Joan Welsh, *writer*

Influence is like a savings account. The less you use it, the more you've got.
—Andrew Young, *politician and pastor*

Who shall set a limit to the influence of a human being?
—Ralph Waldo Emerson, *essayist and poet*

Nothing you do for children is ever wasted. They seem not to notice us, hovering, averting our eyes, and they seldom offer thanks, but what we do for them is never wasted.
—Garrison Keillor, *storyteller, humorist, and radio personality*

How lucky [she] was to have this mother of hers, this constant, reliable, if at times irritating presence in her life—this mother, like so many other mothers, beloved and blamed. Lucky she was to have experienced, through her mother, the twisted intricacies of deep, and deeply complex, love.

—*Daphne Kalotay, novelist*

All daughters, even when most aggravated by their mothers, have a secret respect for them.

—*Phyllis Bottoms, novelist*

When your mother asks, "Do you want a piece of advice?" it's a mere formality. It doesn't matter if you answer yes or no. You're going to get it anyway.

—*Erma Bombeck, writer and humorist*

Don't be discouraged if your children reject your advice. Years later they will offer it to their own offspring.

—*Anonymous*

As mothers, we are building great cathedrals. We cannot be seen if we're doing it right. And one day, it is very possible that the world will marvel, not only at what we have built, but at the beauty that has been added to the world by the sacrifices of invisible women.

—Nicole Johnson, writer

Parents are always more knowledgeable than their children, and children are always smarter than their parents.

—Jonathan Safran Foer, novelist

The miracle of children is that we just don't know how they will change or who they will become.

—Eileen Kennedy-Moore, writer and psychologist

Line up all the days of childhood, a freeze-frame from every day. Side by side most days look very much the same. But flip ahead through the months, the years, and the big picture emerges. The child grows up. The newborn becomes a toddler, who becomes a child, who becomes a teenager, who eventually becomes an adult. You can't pinpoint any single day that change happens—time creeps up on us that way—but it does, and it's irreversible. We can't hoard time. We can't stall it. We shouldn't dwell on its passing. What can we do? Spend time with our children now. Make the time meaningful. Be generous, deep-pocketed with time spent. Make it fun. Enjoy it. It's an investment.

Love the moment, and the energy of that moment will spread beyond all boundaries.

—*Sister Corita Kent, artist and educator*

[T]he film of childhood can never be run through for a second showing.

—*Evelyn Nown, writer*

The three-year-old is lost at five, the five-year-old at nine. We consort with ghosts, even as we sit and eat with, scold and kiss, their current corporeal forms. We speak to people who have vanished and, when they answer us, they do the same.

—*Karen Joy Fowler, novelist*

Children are natural Zen masters; their world is brand new in each and every moment.

—*John Bradshaw, educator and counselor*

I sit down on the bed, cradling her little head against my shoulder, inhaling her sweet baby scent. . . . Right now she is pure and undiminished and beautiful.

—Jonathan Tropper, *novelist*

Parenting: the days are long but the years are short.

—Anonymous

The bittersweet side of appreciating life's most precious moments is the unbearable awareness that those moments are passing.

—Marc Parent, writer

Children have neither past nor future; and, what scarcely ever happens to us, they enjoy the present.

—Jean de La Bruyère, essayist

The work will wait
while you show the
child the rainbow,
but the rainbow
won't wait while you
do the work.

—*Patricia Clafford,
writer*

Yesterday is gone.
Tomorrow has not
yet come. We have
only today.
Let us begin.

—**Anonymous**

The universe is a strange, strange place
when all of a sudden you can't use
your glass with the Bionic Woman on it
any more.

—*Heather O'Neill, novelist and journalist*

Oh, but she never wanted James to grow a day older or Cam either. These two she would have liked to keep for ever just as the way they were, demons of wickedness, angels of delight, never to see them grow up into long-legged monsters.

—Virginia Woolf, novelist and publisher

While I nurse you to sleep I take stock. I turn over in my mind, the contents of the fridge, the washing on the floor, the money in the bank. I count up the years I've had so far and the years I might have left. I work out how old I will be—seventy two—when you are the age I am now—thirty seven. I hope I make it. I count the eggs you already have in your body and those I have in mine and I wonder at the people they may become. I think about the person I was before I met you, the life I led, the things I've gained and the things I've lost, I count them all.

—Milli Hill, writer

We are not the same persons this year as last; nor are those we love. It is a happy chance if we, changing, continue to love a changed person.

—W. Somerset Maugham, playwright and novelist

I know I can't make time slow down, can't hold our life as it is in a freeze frame or slow my children's inexorable journeys into adulthood and lives of their own. But I can celebrate those journeys by bearing witness to them, by paying attention, and, perhaps most of all, by carrying on with my own growth and becoming. . . . I will not waste this life, not one hour, not one minute.

—*Katrina Kenison, editor and writer*

I live in the moment. If I am in the boardroom then I am in the boardroom and if I am at my son's soccer match, I am at my son's soccer match. Whatever I am doing I live totally in that moment.

—*Gail Kelly, banking chief executive officer*

[A]s they grow and develop, they change. No sooner have you figured out how to relate well to one situation than they grow out of that and into something you've never seen before. You have to be continually mindful and present that you aren't lingering with a view of things that no longer applies.

—*Jon Kabat-Zinn, spiritual teacher*

There are random moments—tossing a salad, coming up the driveway to the house, ironing the seams flat on a quilt square, standing at the kitchen window and looking out at the delphiniums, hearing a burst of laughter from one of my children's rooms—when I feel a wavelike rush of joy. This is my true religion: arbitrary moments of nearly painful happiness for a life I feel privileged to lead.

—*Elizabeth Berg, novelist*

Motherhood is not a hobby. It is a calling. You do not collect children because you find them cuter than stamps. It is not something you can do if you can squeeze the time in. It is what God gave you time for.

—*Elder Neil Andersen, religious leader*

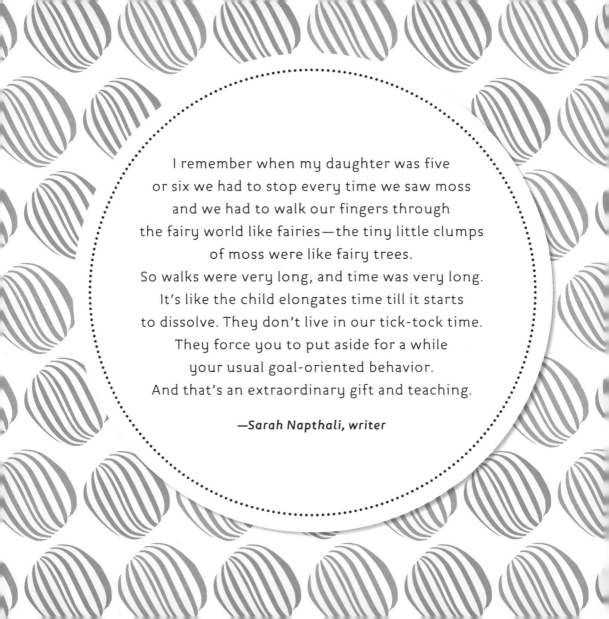

I remember when my daughter was five
or six we had to stop every time we saw moss
and we had to walk our fingers through
the fairy world like fairies—the tiny little clumps
of moss were like fairy trees.
So walks were very long, and time was very long.
It's like the child elongates time till it starts
to dissolve. They don't live in our tick-tock time.
They force you to put aside for a while
your usual goal-oriented behavior.
And that's an extraordinary gift and teaching.

—Sarah Napthali, *writer*

I hated going to the playground EVERY DAY. If someone had only told me it wouldn't last forever.

—*Nancy Woodruff, novelist and educator*

The best inheritance a parent can give his children is a few minutes of his time each day.

—*Orlando A. Battista, chemist and writer*

In family life, be completely present.

—*Lao Tzu, philosopher*

I never hear parents exclaim impatiently, "Children, you must not make so much noise," that I do not think how soon the time may come when, beside the vacant seat, those parents would give all the world, could they hear once more the ringing laughter which once so disturbed them.

—*A. E. Kittredge, religious leader*

In terms of days and moments lived, you'll never again be as young as you are right now, so spend this day, the youth of your future, in a way that deflects regret. Invest in yourself. Have some fun. Do something important. Love somebody extra. In one sense, you're just a kid, but a kid with enough years on her to know that every day is priceless.

—Victoria Moran, writer and spiritual teacher

If you want to get a child to love you, then you should just go hide in the closet for three or four hours. They get down on their knees and pray for you to return. That child will turn you into God. Lonely children probably wrote the Bible.

—Heather O'Neill, novelist and journalist

Kids spell love T-I-M-E.

—John Crudele, columnist

This day will not come again.
Each minute is worth a priceless gem.
—Takuan Soho, spiritual leader

A friend of mine with four kids said, "I always tell myself, 'These are the good old days.'" It helps to remember how quickly other stages vanished—like waking up several times in the middle of the night with a newborn. It seemed interminable—but it also flashed by. I keep a one-sentence journal, too, so I can hang on to the little memories that would otherwise get forgotten.

—*Gretchen Rubin, writer and attorney*

Many things can wait; the child cannot. Now is the time his bones are being formed, his mind is being developed. To him we cannot say tomorrow; his name is today.

—*Gabriela Mistral, poet and diplomat*

The darling mispronunciations of childhood!—dear me, there's no music that can touch it; and how one grieves when it wastes away and dissolves into correctness, knowing it will never visit his bereaved ear again.

—Mark Twain, *novelist and humorist*

[My son] has taught me the joy of being present in the moment and letting go of the stresses for 30 seconds or three minutes, and engaging and listening.

—*Julie Sokol, partner at Accenture*

If I cannot give my children a perfect mother I can at least give them more of the one they've got—and make that one more loving. I will be available. I will take time to listen, time to play, time to be home when they arrive from school, time to counsel and encourage.

—Ruth Bell Graham, *wife of religious leader Billy Graham*

It will be gone before you know it. The fingerprints on the wall appear higher and higher. Then suddenly they disappear.

—Dorothy Evslin, *writer and educator*

Parents are so busy with
the physical rearing of children
that they miss the glory of
parenthood, just as the grandeur
of the trees is lost
when raking leaves.

✢ ✢ ✢

—Marcelene Cox, writer

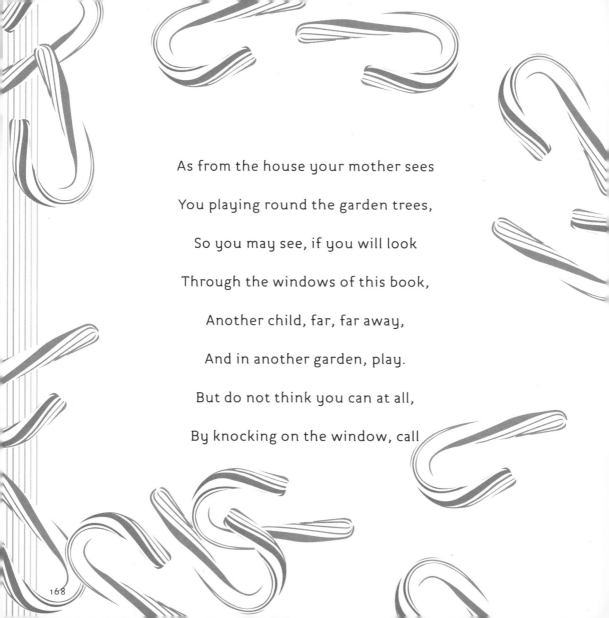

As from the house your mother sees

You playing round the garden trees,

So you may see, if you will look

Through the windows of this book,

Another child, far, far away,

And in another garden, play.

But do not think you can at all,

By knocking on the window, call

That child to hear you. He intent

Is all on his play-business bent.

He does not hear; he will not look,

Nor yet be lured out of this book.

For, long ago, the truth to say,

He has grown up and gone away,

And it is but a child of air

That lingers in the garden there.

—Robert Louis Stevenson, novelist and poet,
from "To Any Reader"

Cleaning and scrubbing can wait till tomorrow . . . for babies grow up we've learned to our sorrow . . . so quiet down cobwebs . . . dust go to sleep . . . I'm rocking my baby because babies don't keep!

—*Anonymous*

Embrace the moment before it escapes from our grasp. For the only promise of childhood, of any childhood, is that it will someday end. And in the end, we must ask ourselves what we have given our children to take its place. And is it enough?

—*Richard Paul Evans, novelist*

For every human soul there must surely be a possible childhood worth living, but once it slips by, there isn't any reclaiming it or revising it.

—*Gregory Maguire, novelist*

Personally, when we're feeling exasperated, we like to think in terms of "the last time"—as in, there will be a last time for everything. When will be the last time I give her a bottle, or the last time I put her to bed in her crib, or the last time I can actually cradle my son in my lap, or the last time he will let me hold his hand in public? It's amazing how quickly this puts things in perspective.

—Trisha Ashworth and Amy Nobile, writers

When you pause to *think* what children mean to you, of course they make you feel good. The problem is, 95 percent of the time, you're not thinking about what they mean to you. You're thinking that you have to take them to piano lessons.

—Daniel Gilbert, psychologist

Time is your most precious gift because you only have a set amount of it. You can make more money, but you can't make more time. When you give someone your time, you are giving them a portion of your life that you'll never get back. Your time is your life. That is why the greatest gift you can give someone is your time.

—Rick Warren, minister and writer

Time does not really exist for mothers, with regard to their children. It does not matter greatly how old the child is—in the blink of an eye, a mother can see the child again as they were when they were born, when they learned how to walk, as they were at any age—at any time, even when the child is fully grown or a parent themselves.

—Diana Gabaldon, novelist and ecologist

[PARENTS] CAN RESIST THE IMPULSE TO "PROVE" THEIR **LOVE** BY SHOWERING CHILDREN WITH THINGS THEY DO NOT NEED AND GIVE THEM **PRECIOUS TIME** AND **ATTENTION** INSTEAD.

—HILLARY RODHAM CLINTON,
U.S. SECRETARY OF STATE

What mother doesn't teeter at times? On one hand is the fantasy of being a perfect parent, and on the other are all our other ambitions: career, creative outlets, spiritual growth, friendship and romance, and so on. How to balance it all? Inspiration comes with the assurance that we can flourish within limitations—even when we're unsteady. And contentment comes in the knowledge that there's really no such thing as a sustained perfect equilibrium. Every day is a push and pull. The good news is that, on balance, we can do more than we think—if we throw our weight around.

Thus far the mighty mystery of motherhood is this: How is it that doing it all feels like nothing is ever getting done?

—*Rebecca Woolf, writer*

Life is like riding a bicycle. To keep your balance, you must keep moving.

—*Albert Einstein, theoretical physicist*

If evolution really works, how come mothers only have two hands?

—*Milton Berle, comedian and actor*

Feel no guilt. Getting married and giving birth does not mean that you have sold your life away to perfectly healthy people who can get their own damn socks.

—*Jennifer Crusie, novelist*

When I had my daughter, I learned what the sound of one hand clapping is—it's a woman holding an infant in one arm and a pen in the other.

—Kate Braverman, writer

Repeat after me. There. Is. No. Such. Thing. As Balance.... A decade of motherhood and too many missteps and mistakes to count have since given me the wisdom to give up the stupid balance myth once and for all.... I came to realize that what I wanted all along wasn't really balance after all. It's fulfillment.

—*Brooke Burke, actor and model*

Women do not have to sacrifice personhood if they are mothers. They do not have to sacrifice motherhood in order to be persons. Liberation was meant to expand women's opportunities, not to limit them. The self-esteem that has been found in new pursuits can also be found in mothering.

—Elaine Heffner, writer

In France, you can be
a very involved mother *and* have interests
and take time away from your kids.
In fact, it's better for both the mother
and child to have some separate space.

—*Pamela Druckerman, journalist*

Advice to fellow mothers in the same boat.
"How do you do it all?" Crack a joke.
Make it seem easy. Make everything seem easy.
Make life seem easy and
parenthood and marriage.

—*Rebecca Woolf, writer*

Instant availability without continuous presence is probably the best role a mother can play.

—*Lotte Bailyn, professor*

I'm way more focused, because my time is very limited. In the time that I have, I need to get done what needs to be done and I find that I am way more efficient.

—*Rachel Zoe, fashion stylist and television host*

The essential question is not, "How busy are you?" but "What are you busy at?"

—*Oprah Winfrey, talk show host, actor, and philanthropist*

Jugglers invariably drop balls, and no matter the persistent criticism of the Bad Mother police, balls do bounce. When they fall, all you need to do is pick them up and throw them back in the air.

—*Ayelet Waldman, lawyer and writer*

I have become more selective too. How much time I will spend outside on the street, whom to meet when, you become more selective about these because now you are doing many more things at once. So you start to use your time more wisely.

—*Elif Shafak, novelist*

[Motherhood is] a choice you make every day, to put someone else's happiness and well-being ahead of your own, to teach the hard lessons, to do the right thing even when you're not sure what the right thing is . . . and to forgive yourself, over and over again, for doing everything wrong.

—*Donna Ball, novelist*

I used to put [my daughter] into the pushchair [stroller] and walk her around Edinburgh, wait until she nodded off and then hurry to a cafe and write as fast as I could. It's amazing how much you can get done when you know you have very limited time. I've probably never been as productive since, if you judge by words per hour.

—*J. K. Rowling, novelist*

Whatever you're doing, do it 100 percent. If you're with the kids, don't think about work, and if you're at work, don't think about home. But the most important thing is to put family first.

—Ann Curry, television news journalist

You're not managing an inconvenience; you're raising a human being.

—Kittie Frantz, nurse and educator

If you have three or four—or more—chickabiddies, you're dancing on a hot griddle all the time. You don't have time to think about anything else. And if you've only got one or two, it's almost harder. You have room left over—empty spaces that you think you've got to fill up.

—Sharon Creech, novelist

My mom used to say it doesn't matter how many kids you have . . . because one kid'll take up 100% of your time so more kids can't possibly take up more than 100% of your time.

—*Karen Brown, writer*

Motherhood has a very humanizing effect. Everything gets reduced to essentials.

—*Meryl Streep, actor*

Being asked to decide between your passion for work and your passion for children was like being asked by your doctor whether you preferred him to remove your brain or your heart.

—*Mary Kay Blakely, writer and professor*

The phrase "working mother" is redundant.

—*Jane Sellman, writer and professor*

It's not always easy, but I find that when I approach each piece of my life—writing, laundry, negotiating sibling scuffles—as a creative act, I feel much less guilt around the pull between the two aspects of myself. Reminding myself that I am still creating my life and my family's memories even when I'm not creating art helps me feel more fulfilled.

—*Miki DeVivo, artist*

I remember breaking down in our pediatrician's office one day because I was worried my children were somehow suffering for my occasional absences. The pediatrician could see how upset I was. He looked me right in the eyes and said, "I've got a daughter about your age in med school. I would never tell her not to dream her dreams, and give up on everything she wants to be and can be, simply because she was born female. Your children are wonderful. They are flourishing."

—*Susan Lucci, actor and television host*

For our sense of ourselves, and for our children's sense of how life really works— it seems important to make sure kids know that what their mother does is as essential as buckling on He-Man's armor.

—Francine Prose, novelist

I can't spend as much time with my guitar or doing my thing or going deep into something. At first I was resistant to that, but then I realized that [motherhood is] the best thing that ever happened to my relationship and my work. . . . It's really kind of refreshed my love of what I do, to step back from it.

—*Ani DiFranco, singer-songwriter*

Since I'm a mother and a wife, I have to have passion or the frustration would win out.

—*Andrea Jung, chairman and CEO of Avon*

I also want them to know work is really fun for me—"Hey, look what I get to do!" As opposed to feeling like, Oh, I'm a terrible mother.

—*Gwyneth Paltrow, actor and singer*

Working is taking care of your children: It's paying for dental care, it's putting money in the bank for their college fund, it's making sure they have enough good food to eat.

—Ann Curry, television news journalist

You aren't a terrible parent if you aren't there after work every day baking cookies......We just have to realize we're not doing our children a disservice when we're engaged in our jobs if we are also engaged in them.

—Elizabeth Blackburn, molecular biologist and Nobel Laureate

I looked on child rearing not only as a work of love and duty but as a profession that was fully as interesting and challenging as any honorable profession in the world and one that demanded the best I could bring to it.

—Rose Kennedy, philanthropist

If I were to choose among all gifts and qualities that which, on the whole, makes life pleasantest, I should select the love of children. No circumstance can render this world wholly solitude to one who has this possession.

—T. W. Higginson, minister

I think that saving a little child
And bringing him to his own,
Is a derned sight better business
Than loafing around the throne.
—John Hay, poet

In my previous life I was a civil attorney. At one point I truly believed that was what I wanted to be—but that was before I'd been handed a fistful of crushed violets from a toddler.

—Jodi Picoult, novelist

You are never the same person before and after you have children. I guess when I do get to work, I feel so appreciative of it because I don't get to do it all the time. [Motherhood has] made much more clear lines of my life and my work and I deeply appreciate it.

—Uma Thurman, actor

Motherhood diffuses me into a mist and work clarifies the margins.

—Carmen Giménez Smith, writer

For me the best moment is when your child gets older and tells you that they value what you have done, rather than you being always with them. When [my son] was 11, he said that to me—it was a very important moment for me.

—Christine Lagarde, lawyer and managing director of the International Monetary Fund

The most important thing
she'd learned over the years was
that there was no way to be a
perfect mother and
a million ways to be a good one.

✣ ✣ ✣

—Jill Churchill, writer

Humor is armor. It's how we mothers protect ourselves from the absurdities and frustrations of child-raising. There's a bright side to sleepless nights, bickering, pant-tugging, eye-rolling, and name-calling. There's a way to cope with messes and blowouts. Savor some of the nuttiness, and it all goes down more smoothly. Give yourself a moment of reflection. We need a sense of humor; so much of a parent's day is touchingly exasperating, patently absurd. Funny thing is, we may even start to enjoy the lumps.

Families are like fudge—mostly sweet with a few nuts.

—*Anonymous*

A sense of humor gets you through just about anything.

—*Julia Louis-Dreyfus, actor*

Humor helps us to think out of the box. The average child laughs about 400 times per day, the average adult laughs only 15 times per day. What happened to the other 385 laughs?

—*Anonymous*

Sometimes the laughter in mothering is the recognition of the ironies and absurdities. Sometimes, though, it's just pure, unthinking delight.

—*Barbara Schapiro, writer*

We spend the first twelve months of our children's lives teaching them to walk and talk and the next twelve telling them to sit down and shut up.

—*Phyllis Diller, actor and comedian*

Laughter and tears are both responses to frustration and exhaustion. . . . I myself prefer to laugh, since there is less cleaning up to do afterward.

—*Kurt Vonnegut Jr., novelist*

Having children is like living in a frat house—nobody sleeps, everything's broken, and there's a lot of throwing up.

—**Ray Romano, actor and comedian**

You know you're a mother when your child throws up and you run to catch it before it hits the rug.

—**Anonymous**

It is amazing how quickly the kids learn to drive a car, yet are unable to understand the lawn mower, snowblower, or vacuum cleaner.

—**Ben Bergor, actor**

Anyone who thinks the art of conversation is dead ought to tell a child to go to bed.

—*Robert Gallagher, writer*

There are only two things a child will share willingly—communicable diseases and his mother's age.

—*Benjamin Spock, pediatrician*

The real menace in dealing with a five-year-old is that in no time at all you begin to sound like a five-year-old.

—*Jean Kerr, writer and playwright*

Any kid will run any errand for you if you ask at bedtime.

—**Red Skelton, comedian**

Sleep is out ... tired is the new black.

—*Amy Poehler, actor and comedian*

Spies and parents never sleep.

—**Linda Gerber, novelist**

Parents: persons who spend half their time worrying how a child will turn out, and the rest of the time wondering when a child will turn in.

—**Ted Cook, comedian**

Insomnia: A contagious disease often transmitted from babies to parents.

—**Shannon Fife, writer and director**

When we weren't scratching each other's eyes out,
we were making each other laugh harder than anyone
else could.

—Lucie Arnaz, singer and actress

Against the assault of laughter nothing can stand.
—Mark Twain, novelist and humorist

Insanity is hereditary: You can get it from your children.
—Sam Levinson, actor and director

Mothers are all slightly insane.

—J. D. Salinger, novelist

No matter how calmly you try to referee, parenting will eventually produce bizarre behavior, and I'm not talking about the kids.

—Bill Cosby, comedian, actor, and educator

Home is wherever my bunch of crazies are.

—Anonymous

Any child can tell you that the sole purpose of a middle name is so he can tell when he's really in trouble.

—Dennis Fakes, writer

That's what children are for—that their parents may not be bored.

—Ivan Turgenev, novelist

Having one child
makes you a parent;
having two
you are a referee.

**—David Frost, *journalist
and comedian***

Children aren't
happy with nothing
to ignore, and
that's what parents
were created for.

—*Ogden Nash, poet*

There are times when parenthood
seems nothing more than feeding the
hand that bites you.

—*Ann Diehl, writer*

There are three ways to get something done: do it yourself, employ someone, or forbid your children to do it.

—*Mona Crane, writer*

If you can laugh at it, you can live with it.

—**Erma Bombeck, writer and humorist**

Yes, I'm paranoid—but am I paranoid *enough*?

—**David Foster Wallace, novelist**

The mind, placed before any kind of difficulty, can find an ideal outlet in the absurd. Accommodation to the absurd readmits adults to the mysterious realm inhabited by children.

—*André Breton, writer and poet*

Raising kids is part joy and part guerilla warfare.

—**Ed Asner, actor**

Like all parents, my husband and I just do the best we can, and hold our breath, and hope we've set aside enough money to pay for our kids' therapy.

—*Michelle Pfeiffer, actor*

Look around you. Everywhere. They are there. In every home—lurking in dark corners . . . small, bipedal entities with almost human brains play their games in which adults are the pawns. They play and wait for the time when they will take over the world!

—*John Blair Moore, comic book writer*

Of course I don't always enjoy being a mother. At those times my husband and I hole up somewhere in the wine country, eat, drink, make mad love and pretend we were born sterile and raise poodles.

—*Dorothy DeBolt, speaker and parenting expert*

A child embarrassed by his mother . . . is just a child who hasn't lived long enough.

—*Mitch Albom, writer, journalist, and broadcaster*

Children are a great comfort in your old age, and they help you reach it faster, too.

—*Lionel Kauffman, writer*

There is no reciprocity. Men love women, women love children, children love hamsters.

—*Alice Thomas Ellis, writer*

I will continue to freak out my children by knitting in public. It's good for them.

—*Stephanie Pearl-McPhee, writer and lactation consultant*

When those eyes meet your eyes—I was feeling things I never had feelings like before. I never loved anyone so much at first meeting. I love her so much! But! Let's make no mistake why these babies come here: to replace us. Their first words are "Mama," "Dada," and "Bye-bye." We'll see who's wearing the diapers when this is all over.

—*Jerry Seinfeld, comedian, actor, and producer*

If you've never been hated by your child, you've never been a parent.

—*Bette Davis, actor*

Sing out loud in the car even, or especially, if it embarrasses your children.

—**Marilyn Penland, writer**

It is impossible for you
to be angry and laugh at the
same time. Anger and laughter
are mutually exclusive and
you have the power
to choose either.

✤ ✤ ✤

—*Wayne Dyer, self-help advocate*

Ask not only what you can do for your child, but what your child does for you. Mothers give a lot, but we also receive—and the gifts are priceless. What do we get? The gifts of purpose and meaning. The gift of wonder. The gift of courage. The gifts of empathy and freedom from self-absorption. The gift of grounding. Usefulness, well-roundedness, diplomacy, and contentment—all gifts. Even the gift of righting the wrongs from our own pasts. Perhaps best of all, children can offer us the gift of hope for the future. When feeling drained, draw on these gifts.

Kids are life's only guaranteed, bona fide upside surprise.

—*Jack Nicholson, actor*

We can see that the baby is as much an instrument of nourishment for us as we are for him.

—*Polly Berrien Berends, spiritual teacher*

The soul is healed by being with children.

—*Fyodor Dostoevsky, novelist*

What children take from us, they give. When we are not totally "free," we learn how to cope with a smaller world, less time, less luxury, . . . We become people who feel more deeply, question more deeply, and love more deeply.

—*Sonia Taitz, novelist*

At this stage of my life, I've finally come to realize I've learned more from my children than they ever learned from me.

—*C. J. Heck, poet*

I brought children into this dark world because it needed the light that only a child can bring.

—*Liz Armbruster, writer*

Sitting in the pre-kindergarten room yesterday for a Mother's Day Tea was so cute. When the teacher asked what gift the kids could give their mothers, one child responded, "Me!" All of the mothers responded with, "Ahhhhhh!" If we can truly understand that explanation, we can be better mothers.

—*Kristin Gembala, educator and entrepreneur*

Blessed be childhood, which brings down something of heaven into the midst of our rough earthliness.

—*Henri Frédéric Amiel, philosopher*

No one has yet fully realized the wealth of sympathy, kindness and generosity hidden in the soul of a child. The effort of every true education should be to unlock that treasure.

—*Emma Goldman, author*

You can learn many things from children. How much patience you have, for instance.

—*Franklin P. Jones, reporter and executive*

Parents learn a lot from their children about coping with life.

—*Muriel Spark, novelist*

[When] you're dying laughing because your three-year-old made a fart joke, it doesn't matter what else is going on. That's real happiness.

—*Gwyneth Paltrow, actor and singer*

You give me a sense of place in this world. I belong somewhere unquestionably. I belong to you. . . . It lets me be both young again and a grown and mature woman. What I give to you, I give to me too. . . . I feel so important to your life, your well-being, your very survival, and that feeling allows me to feel important too. I feel useful and vital each and every day.

—*Tian Dayton, clinical psychologist and author*

Observing the fearless and loving way in which a child embraces nature and people, freed me and pushed me in the right direction.

—*Susannah Martin, artist*

My relationship with death used to be far more ambivalent . . . now it's very much about staying in the world.

—*Nicole Kidman, actor and producer*

A baby is God's opinion that the world should go on.

—*Carl Sandburg, poet*

Children are a wonderful gift. They have an extraordinary capacity to see into the heart of things and to expose sham and humbug for what they are.

—Desmond Tutu, activist and bishop

You become a fulfilled human being when you become responsible for a young person. Everything you do and say is a reflection of this little person who is also a reflection of yourself. I see the simplicity in your eyes and realize that you have become my teacher and I your student. You have made me value the most basic things in life.

—Cristina Perez, television host

The real voyage of discovery consists not in seeking new landscapes, but in having new eyes.

—Marcel Proust, novelist

All the time a person is a child he is both a child and learning to be a parent. After he becomes a parent he becomes predominantly a parent reliving childhood.

—Benjamin Spock, pediatrician

One reason we have children I think is to learn that parts of ourselves we had given up for dead are merely dormant and that the old joys can reemerge fresh and new and in a completely different form.

—*Anne Fadiman, novelist*

I wept because I was re-experiencing the enthusiasm of my childhood; I was once again a child, and nothing in the world could cause me harm.

—*Paulo Coelho, lyricist and novelist*

A house is never perfectly furnished for enjoyment unless there is a child in it rising three years old, and a kitten rising three weeks.

—*Robert Southey, poet*

When I look into a child's eyes, I realize how simple life should be.

—*Anonymous*

That's how it is with infants. The minute the pain's gone, so are the tears. If more people would do that, the world would be a happier place.

—*Susan Wiggs, novelist*

Children often can forget their sins and ours as rapidly as hot water removes peanut butter and jelly from faces and hair. Seeing children's ability to change makes some parents realize that change is possible for them as well. Watching how quickly children can give up anger and moods helps us loosen our grip on our own hurts and worries.

—*Nancy Fuchs-Kreimer, rabbi*

Becoming a mom allowed me to just relax in a way I never had before. I used to care A LOT about what I looked like in public, or what people thought of me.

—*Busy Phillips, actor*

All I have to do is see her little smile and know that everything is all right in the world.

—Yolanda Adams, singer

We find a delight in the beauty and happiness of children that makes the heart too big for the body.

—Ralph Waldo Emerson, essayist and poet

When I pick up one of my children and cuddle them, all the strain and stress of life temporarily disappears. There is nothing more wonderful than motherhood and no one will ever love you as much as a small child.

—Nicola Horlick, financier

I said I would get better with each baby, and I have.

—Demi Moore, actor

Most of us have had moments when we touched the divine presence. We did not think it extraordinary because it wasn't; it was just a beautiful moment filled with love. In those simple moments our hearts were alive, and we saw the poignant beauty of life vividly with wonder and appreciation.

—David McArthur, minister

Your children are the greatest gift God will give to you, and their souls the heaviest responsibility He will place in your hands. Take time with them, teach them to have faith in God. Be a person in whom they can have faith. When you are old, nothing else you've done will have mattered as much.

—Lisa Wingate, writer

Parenting is a mirror that forces you to look at yourself. If you can learn from what you observe, you just may have a chance to keep growing yourself.

—Jon Kabat-Zinn, spiritual teacher

IN A HOUSEFUL OF
TODDLERS AND PETS,
YOU CAN START OUT
HAVING A BAD DAY,
BUT YOU KEEP
GETTING DETOURED.

—ROBERT BRAULT, WRITER

I feel more secure and confident [since I became a mother]. I have more patience and am more open to people. It really changes the way you carry yourself and see the world.

—*Adrianna Lima, supermodel*

Having a baby dragged me, kicking and screaming, from the world of self-absorption.

—*Paul Reiser, comedian and actor*

Can you tell me that you cannot smile? Think of the baby, and smile for him, for her, for the future generations. Please don't tell me that a smile and your sorrow just don't go together. It's your sorrow, but what about your baby? It's not his sorrow, it's not her sorrow.

—*Thich Nhat Hanh, monk, poet, and activist*

There are lots of things that you can brush under the carpet about yourself until you're faced with somebody whose needs won't be put off.

—*Angela Carter, novelist and journalist*

My children and their needs saved me from being completely consumed by the devastating emotions dredged up while I wrote. At 3 every afternoon, I had to come out from behind the door and be their mommy again.

—*Kate Moses, novelist*

It seems to me that since I've had children, I've grown richer and deeper. They may have slowed down my writing for awhile, but when I did write, I had more of a self to speak from.

—*Anne Tyler, novelist*

Motherhood has taught me mindfulness.

—*Gwyneth Paltrow, actor and singer*

After the pregnancy, I felt liberated. I learned to accept my body and to give less importance to my appearance.

—*Jessica Alba, actor*

You give up your self, and finally you don't even mind. You become your child's guide to life at the expense of that swollen ego you thought so immutable. I wouldn't have missed this for anything, [Motherhood] humbled my ego and stretched my soul. It awakened me to eternity. It made me know my own humanity, my own mortality, my own limits. It gave me whatever crumbs of wisdom I possess today.

—*Erica Jong, novelist*

My priorities have completely shifted now that my identity is no longer solely wrapped up in myself.

—**Jodie Foster, actor**

I actually think motherhood has saved me from my vanity and it's a relief. You find out so quickly what is essential, whereas before I had Roman, I might have spent an hour shopping for makeup and now it doesn't even occur to me.

—**Debra Messing, *actor and comedian***

I can get ready so quickly now. I'm shocked: It used to take me two hours to get ready for everything, and now I'm like, 'We're leaving in 10, let's go!' As long as my son's okay, we're good.

—*Marissa Jaret Winokur, actor and TV host*

In going through birth and bringing a baby into this world my perspective completely changed. I no longer felt disconnected from my body—I became more aware of my mortality and my limited time here. I think now I am able to accept people for who they are and not place my ideals on them. I can also let go of my anxieties about other people judging me.

—*Lily Mae Martin, artist*

[Before motherhood] I was going through life robotically, even though I thought I was a badass, motherfucking, rebel, outside-it-all person. I was still a sheep in many ways. I wasn't a total pig or anything . . . [but] my life was very small-picture.

—*Madonna, singer-songwriter and actor*

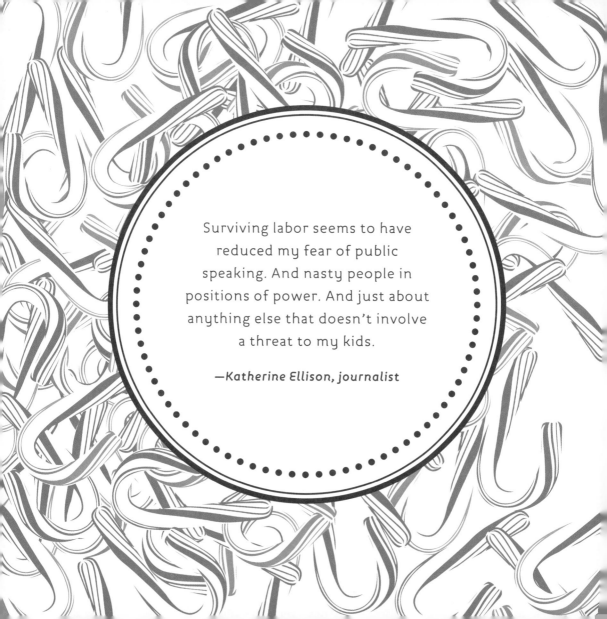

Surviving labor seems to have reduced my fear of public speaking. And nasty people in positions of power. And just about anything else that doesn't involve a threat to my kids.

—*Katherine Ellison, journalist*

No two days are ever the same, which is so exciting.

—*Jada Pinkett Smith, actor and singer-songwriter*

I can tell you that being a mom was great training for the job that I have now. With five kids, there are twenty ways to have an argument. So I acquired certain diplomatic skills, which, I find, are coming in quite handy. They're the ability to head off confrontation, the tactics of distraction and diversion, and just the ability to appreciate the good mood that somebody might be in at any given time.

—*Nancy Pelosi, speaker of the U.S. House of Representatives*

We find ourselves in the sacrifices we make.

—*Cammie McGovern, novelist*

One of the most enriching things for our brains is novelty. New connections are made with novelty, and every day there's something new with the kids.

—*Kelly Lambert, behavioral neuroscientist*

I don't take as much crap as I used to. You know, once you give birth, once you have kids, you realize what's important in life, and you realize it's really not difficult to be a good person.

—*Pamela Anderson, actor*

Motherhood stopped me from being self-destructive.

—*Angelina Jolie, actor*

Children are our second chance to have a great parent-child relationship.

—*Laura Schlessinger, talk show host*

You didn't have a choice about the parents you inherited, but you do have a choice about the kind of parent you will be.

—*Marian Wright Edelman, activist*

Parenthood . . . It's about guiding the next generation, and forgiving the last.

—*Peter Krause, actor and director*

It's never too late to have a happy childhood.

—*Tom Robbins, novelist*

I never had the power to heal a wound with a kiss before you.

—*Anonymous*

It's not only children who grow. Parents do too. As much as we watch to see what our children do with their lives, they are watching us to see what we do with ours. I can't tell my children to reach for the sun. All I can do is reach for it, myself.

—*Joyce Maynard, novelist*

Children are the anchors that hold a mother to life.

—*Sophocles, playwright*

While we try to teach our children all about life,
Our children teach us what life is all about.
—*Angela Schwindt, writer*

It would be difficult to exaggerate the degree to which we are influenced by those we influence.

—*Eric Hoffer, social writer*

A child seldom needs a good talking to as a good listening to.

—*Robert Brault, writer*

There's nothing that can help you understand your beliefs more than trying to explain them to an inquisitive child.

—*Frank A. Clark, minister*

A child's eyes, those clear wells of undefiled thought—what on earth can be more beautiful? Full of hope, love and curiosity, they meet your own. In prayer, how earnest; in joy, how sparkling; in sympathy, how tender! The man who never tried the companionship of a little child has carelessly passed by one of the great pleasures of life, as one passes a rare flower without plucking it or knowing its value.

—*Caroline Norton, writer and social activist*

Parents lend children their experience and a vicarious memory; children endow their parents with a vicarious immortality.

—*George Santayana, philosopher*

There is nothing more thrilling in this world, I think, than having a child that is yours, and yet is mysteriously a stranger.

—*Agatha Christie, novelist*

I had no idea that mothering my own child would be so healing to my own sadness from my childhood.

—*Susie Bright, writer and performer*

When a woman is twenty, a child deforms her; when she is thirty, he preserves her, and when forty, he makes her young again.

—*Leon Blum, politician*

A woman's natural protector is less an aged father or tall brother than a very young child.

—*Delphine de Girardin, writer*

NURTURE

Nothing grows without nurture. We nurture children feeding not only their bodies but their minds and souls. Mothers are the soil a child grows in; we're the sun that feeds them, the atmosphere they breathe. We protect them from the fiercest and most bitter winds. Drop by drop, day by day, we irrigate and fertilize. To coax them to grow, we become climbing walls, trellises, pergolas. Raising children requires instinct and trust; sometimes we must throw our caution to the wind. Prudent pruning is the objective; the trick is to apply enough nurture to bear fruit but not interfere with nature.

Nurture to know, Nurture to grow.

—*Anonymous*

Your family and your love must be cultivated like a garden. Time, effort, and imagination must be summoned constantly to keep any relationship flourishing and growing.

—*Jim Rohn, entrepreneur and speaker*

Every mother should be a true artist, who knows how to weave into her child's life images of grace and beauty, the true poet capable of writing on the soul of childhood the harmony of love and truth, and teaching it how to produce the grandest of all poems—the poetry of a true and noble life.

—*Frances Ellen Watkins Harper, writer and activist*

...Open doors to unknown directions to the child so he can explore. Don't make him afraid of the unknown; give him support.

—*Osho, mystic and spiritual teacher*

A child is like an early spring bulb that carries all the resources needed within its skin for the first push through the soil towards the sun. And just as a little bit of water can start the bulb to grow, even through fissured rock, so can a little kindness give a child the ability to push through the dark.

—*Kathleen Kent, novelist*

A woman is the full circle. Within her is the power to create, nurture and transform.

—*Diane Mariechild, spiritual teacher*

Love is the will to extend one's self for the purpose of nurturing one's own or another's spiritual growth. . . . Love is as love does. Love is an act of will—namely, both an intention and an action. Will also implies choice. We do not have to love. We choose to love.

—*M. Scott Peck, psychiatrist*

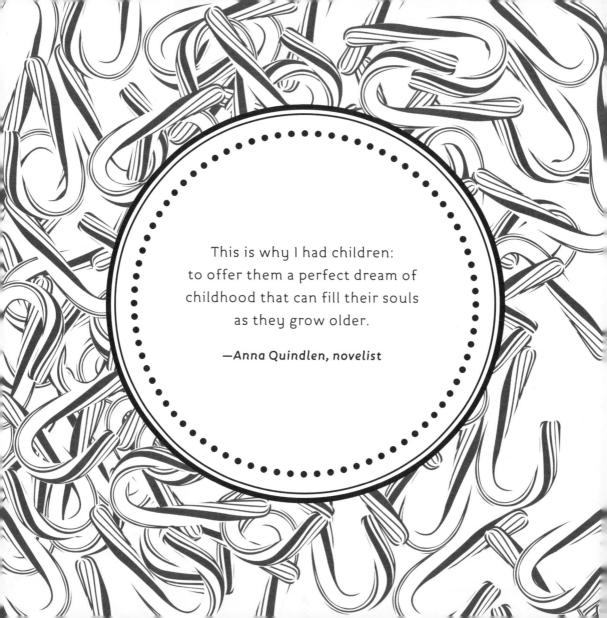

This is why I had children:
to offer them a perfect dream of
childhood that can fill their souls
as they grow older.

—*Anna Quindlen, novelist*

Love does not dominate; it cultivates.

—*Johann Wolfgang von Goethe, poet and polymath*

The climbing plant's fruits are not a burden to it.

—*Sinhalese proverb*

Those who are nurtured best, survive best.

—*Louis Cozolino, psychologist*

The difference between ordinary and extraordinary is that little extra.

—*Jimmy Johnson, coach*

Children need sunlight. . . . They need kindness and refreshment and affection. Every home, regardless of the cost of the house, can provide an environment of love which will be an environment of salvation.

—*Gordon B. Hinckley, religious leader*

Families are designed to nurture the minds, wills, and emotions of its members so that the barriers created by fear of the unknown can be replaced by the confidence that comes from knowing you are loved whether you succeed or fail.

—*Leigh A. Bortins, writer*

Let them know that you're always there, but don't hold them in the house. Let them go. Encourage them to be self-reliant. Give them self-respect.

—*Maya Angelou, poet and novelist*

No matter what else they're doing, women are also always nurturing.

—*Cokie Roberts, news journalist*

The clew of our destiny, wander where we will, lies at the cradle foot.

—*Gerhard Richter, artist*

When I was raising my girls, I often wondered if it was all worth it. I would have these thoughts especially on days when I had put forth extra effort. No one seemed to notice the freshly ironed tablecloth and the flowers on the dining table, or the smell of homemade bread.

I would quickly remind myself that I was building a nest for my children. Someday, each of these little girls would search their hearts and remember what they cherished the most about their own childhood—a mother's touch!

—*Sandra Sage, writer*

A day is Eternity's seed, and we are its Gardeners.
—*Erika Harris, writer*

Scientists have shown that high nurturing—from any loving, trust-inducing adult—may make babies smarter, healthier, and better able to deal with stress. These are qualities they will carry throughout their lives and into the lives of their own children.

—*Louann Brizendine, neuropsychiatrist and writer*

Be careful what you water your dreams with. Water them with worry and fear and you will produce weeds that choke the life from your dream. Water them with optimism and solutions and you will cultivate success.

—*Lao Tzu, philosopher*

There is no nature that exists devoid of nurture; there is no nurture that develops without nature. To say otherwise is like saying that the area of a field is determined by its length but not its width. Every behavior is the product of an instinct trained by experience.

—*Matt Ridley, scientist and writer*

The hardest part of raising a child is teaching them to ride bicycles. A shaky child on a bicycle for the first time needs both support and freedom. The realization that this is what the child will always need can hit hard.

—*Sloan Wilson, novelist*

My baby's eyes, in other years,
May fill with many scalding tears;
And yet, through cruel taunts and jeers
A mother's love will banish fears.

—Anonymous

Love is not something we give or get; it is something that we nurture and grow, a connection that can only be cultivated between two people when it exists within each one of them— we can only love others as much as we love ourselves. Shame, blame, disrespect, betrayal, and the withholding of affection damage the roots from which love grows.

—Brené Brown, research professor

All a child's life depends on the ideal it has of its parents. Destroy that and everything goes—morals, behavior, everything.

—E. M. Forster, novelist

A mother's heart is the child's classroom.

—Henry Ward Beecher, clergyman and social reformer

Love is like a precious plant.
You can't just accept it and
leave it in the cupboard or just
think it's going to get on by itself.
You've got to keep on watering it.
You've got to really look after it
and nurture it.

**—John Lennon, musician and
singer-songwriter**

Too many parents make life hard for their children by trying, too zealously, to make it easy for them.

—*Johann Wolfgang von Goethe, poet and polymath*

A woman uses her intelligence to find reasons to support her intuition.

—**G. K. Chesterton, writer**

It's important for survival that children have their own experiences, the kind they learn from. The kind their parents arrange for are not as useful.

—*Garrison Keillor, storyteller, humorist, and radio personality*

When children are loved, they live off trust; their bodies and hearts open up to those who respect and love them, who understand and listen to them.

—*Jean Vanier, philosopher and humanitarian*

The best proof of love is trust.

—*Joyce Brothers, psychologist and television personality*

Few things help an individual more than to place responsibility upon him, and to let him know that you trust him.

—Booker T. Washington, educator and orator

Often the things that would scare me, I found, had no basis in truth at all; my child had an inner compass that seemed to keep him safe. Each time he conquered a situation safely I'd give him good feedback and reinforce the part of him that guided him safely around his world. This called for more time and attention, but to me it was worth it, to see the looks of triumph on his face.

—Vimala McClure, writer and spiritual teacher

Respect the child. Wait and see the new product of Nature. Nature loves analogies, but not repetitions. Respect the child. Be not too much his parent. Trespass not on his solitude.

—Ralph Waldo Emerson, essayist and poet

I was a dreaming forest tree,
You were a wild, sweet bird
Who sheltered at the heart of me
Because the north wind stirred;
How, when the chiding gale was still,
When peace fell soft on fear,
You stayed one golden hour to fill
My dream with singing, dear.
To-night the self-same songs are sung
The first green forest heard;
My heart and the gray world grow young—
To shelter you, my bird.
—Sophie Jewett, poet, from "To a Child"

Trust Children. Nothing could be more simple, or more difficult. Difficult because to trust children we must first learn to trust ourselves, and most of us were taught as children that we could not be trusted.

—*John Holt, educator*

My mother taught me some basic philosophies of rearing children. One is that you have to trust them. I tried hard never to say "no" if I could possibly say "yes." I think that worked well because it gave my children the feeling that I trusted them and they were responsible to do the best they could.

—*Marjorie Pay Hinckley, writer and spiritual teacher*

It is better to earn the trust and respect of one of your children than to gain notoriety and adulation of the masses.

—Denis Waitley, motivational speaker

It's always exciting for me when I don't get stressed out about something and it works out in the end. Our daughter, for example, was a late talker. . . . We didn't get our knickers in a knot over it and now she speaks perfectly clearly in long sentences and won't stop, so we celebrate victories that come when we're relaxed.

—*Samantha Bee, actor and comedian*

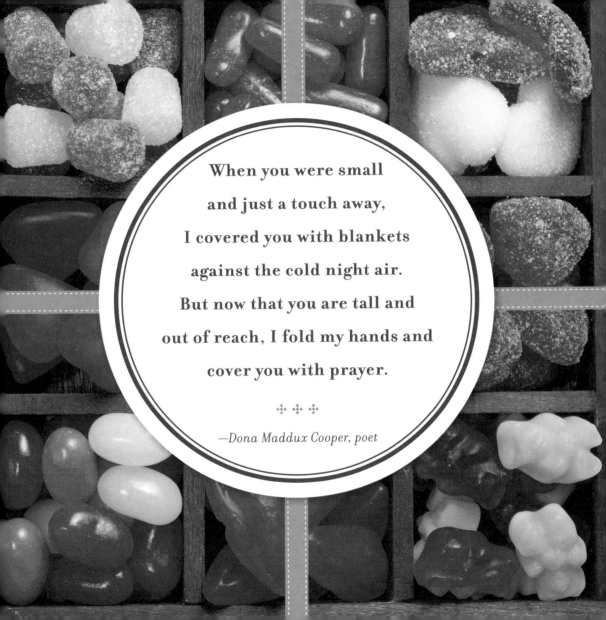

When you were small
and just a touch away,
I covered you with blankets
against the cold night air.
But now that you are tall and
out of reach, I fold my hands and
cover you with prayer.

✣ ✣ ✣

—Dona Maddux Cooper, *poet*

My little three-year-old let the dentist deliver the pain-killing shot and drill extensively into his injured tooth. On a couple of occasions, he said in a little plaintive voice, "I don't like this Mommy!" But when I replied, "You are doing great. I am very proud of you," he lay quietly until the dentist finished his work. I was hit at the time with the realization that what allowed him to do so was his complete faith and trust in me. My eyes filled. I was touched and humbled. I don't think I appreciated the full responsibility of his complete trust until that moment.

—*Ellenore Angelidis, attorney*

Each generation stamps itself onto the next one. The impression is indelible.
Like the flowers in my mother's gardens that come and go with the changing seasons, life re-creates itself.
And the best of life must be nurtured if it is to thrive.

—**Lurlene McDaniel, writer**

What is home? My favorite definition is "a safe place," a place where one is free from attack, a place where one experiences secure relationships and affirmation. It's a place where people share and understand each other. Its relationships are nurturing. The people in it do not need to be perfect; instead, they need to be honest, loving, supportive, recognizing a common humanity that makes all of us vulnerable.

—Gladys Hunt, writer

Before the birth of my first child I worried and worried that I wouldn't be a natural mother, that I wouldn't be able to get it right. I realized eventually that there is no such thing. All of us learn from page one starting on day one—there is no shortcut to learning how to bring up a child, and I don't think you ever stop learning.

—Rowan Coleman, writer

STRENGTH

Motherhood is not for wimps. It takes strength to stand up for our kids—and to stand up to them. Just as motherhood softens our hearts, it also steels our nerves. It strengthens our resolve and forges character. We find ourselves exercising muscles that never existed before—the tongue becomes especially powerful. As defenders and protectors, we're true heavyweights. As empowering as motherhood is, it pushes the limits of endurance. Children are a heart-full and a handful. Parenting—it tests our strength while making us stronger. Mothers have mettle.

Child rearing myth #1: Labor ends when the baby is born.

—*Anonymous*

Motherhood brings as much joy as ever, but it still brings boredom, exhaustion, and sorrow too. Nothing else ever will make you as happy or as sad, as proud or as tired, for nothing is quite as hard as helping a person develop his own individuality especially while you struggle to keep your own.

—*Marguerite Kelly and Elia Parsons, writers*

Birth is not only about making babies. Birth is about making mothers—strong, competent, capable mothers who trust themselves and know their inner strength.

—*Barbara Katz Rothman*

Supermom wasn't a bad job description. The pay was lousy if you were talking about real money. But the payoff was priceless in so many other ways.

—*Roxanne Henke, novelist*

No animal is so inexhaustible as an excited infant.

—*Amy Leslie, actor*

Sometimes the strength of motherhood is greater than natural laws.

—*Barbara Kingsolver, novelist and poet*

I know how to do anything—I'm a Mom.

—*Roseanne Barr, actor and comedian*

Parenthood is what happens when everything is flipped over and spilling everywhere and you can't find a towel or a sponge or your "inside" voice."

—*Kelly Corrigan, novelist*

God did not intend the human family to be wafted to heaven on flowery beds of ease.

—*Frank Knox, editor and publisher*

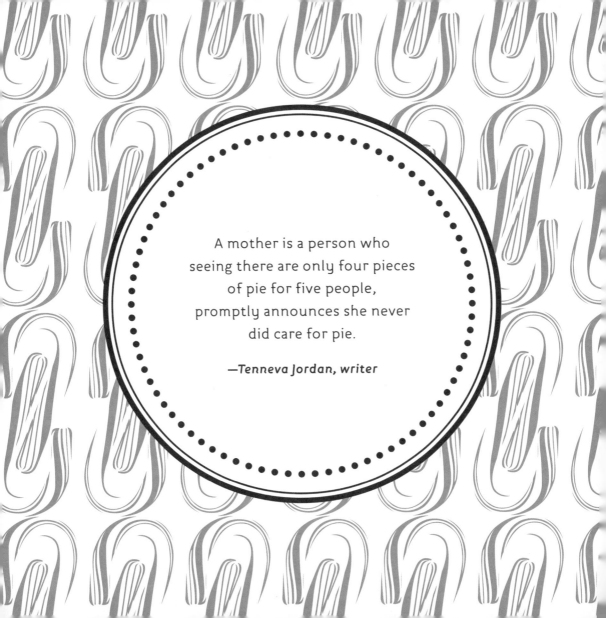

A mother is a person who
seeing there are only four pieces
of pie for five people,
promptly announces she never
did care for pie.

—*Tenneva Jordan, writer*

"What's miraculous about a spider's web?" said Mrs. Arable. "I don't see why you say a web is a miracle—it's just a web."
"Ever try to spin one?"

—E. B. White, novelist

Children are like sponges; they absorb all your strength and leave you limp. . . . But give them a squeeze and you get it all back.

—Barbara Johnson, writer and speaker

The story of a mother's life: Trapped between a scream and a hug.

—Cathy Guisewite, cartoonist

Realize that your life, just like a developing child's, has phases—and now you're in the mommy phase.

—Laura Schlessinger, talk show host

More than any other human relationship, overwhelmingly more, motherhood means being instantly interruptible, responsive, responsible.

—Tillie Olsen, writer

Nobody knows of the work it makes
To keep the home together.
Nobody knows of the steps it takes,
Nobody knows—but Mother.
—Anonymous

Children are a burden to a mother, but not the way a heavy box is to a mule. Our children weigh hard on my heart, and thinking about them growing up honest and healthy, or just living to grow up at all, makes a load in my chest that is bigger than the safe at the bank, and more valuable to me than all the gold inside it.

—Sarah Elliot, writer

Good mothers know all about patience . . . They know that even when patience seems to be at an end, more is required.

—Adaobi Tricia Nwaubani, novelist

There is no point at which you can say, "Well, I'm successful now. I might as well take a nap."

—*Carrie Fisher, actor and novelist*

I know God will not give me anything I can't handle. I just wish He didn't trust me so much.

—*Mother Teresa, nun and Nobel Laureate*

A two-year-old is kind of like having a blender, but you don't have a top for it.

—*Jerry Seinfeld, comedian, actor, and producer*

What mother has never fallen on her knees when she has gone into her son's bedroom and prayed, "Please God. No more. You were only supposed to give me what I could handle."

—*Erma Bombeck, writer and humorist*

Mother's life: it was a race with no finish line.

—*Kristin Hannah, novelist*

A child, like your stomach, doesn't need all you can afford to give it.

—*Frank A. Clark, minister*

Becoming a parent is like joining management: all of a sudden there's no one else to strike against.

—*Ariel Swartley, journalist*

Children are gleeful barbarians.

—*Joseph Morgenstern, critic*

Parents who are afraid to put their foot down usually have children who step on their toes.

—*Chinese proverb*

A child is a curly dimpled lunatic.

—*Ralph Waldo Emerson, essayist and poet*

There was a little girl,
And she had a little curl,
Right in the middle of her forehead;
When she was good she was very, very good,
When she was bad she was horrid.
—Henry Wadsworth Longfellow, poet

A mother's life, you see, is one long succession of dramas, now soft and tender, now terrible. Not an hour but has its joys and fears.

—*Honoré de Balzac, novelist and playwright*

A young lady is a female child who has just done something dreadful.

—Judith Martin, columnist

Motherhood is not for the faint-hearted. Frogs, skinned knees, and the insults of teenage girls are not meant for the wimpy.

—*Danielle Steel, novelist*

Being deeply loved by someone gives you strength, while loving someone deeply gives you courage.

—*Lao Tzu, philosopher*

Of all the haunting moments of motherhood, few rank with hearing your own words come out of your daughter's mouth.

—*Victoria Secunda, psychologist*

Boy, n.: a noise with dirt on it.

—**Anonymous**

Of all the animals, the boy is the most unmanageable.

—**Plato, philosopher**

People with great passions, people who accomplish great deeds, people who possess strong feelings, even people with great minds and a strong personality, rarely come out of good little boys and girls.

—*Lev Vygotsky, psychologist*

The more boring a child is,
the more the parents,
when showing off the child,
receive adulation for being good
parents—because they have a tame
child-creature in their house.

—*Frank Zappa, singer-songwriter*

Reward the good, ignore the bad.

—Zen saying

It's not easy being a mother. If it were easy, fathers would do it.

—"The Golden Girls", television sitcom

The wildest colts make the best horses.

—Plutarch, philosopher

You learn that you can take on quite a lot and make it all work. When your kids need you to be strong and secure, it's very natural to be.

—Heidi Klum, model and fashion designer

The only thing worse than fighting a giant scorpion was fighting a giant scorpion who was trying to protect her young.

—Suzanne Collins, novelist

You drag destruction behind,
a little boy security
blanket; my radio, that older kid's
head you hit with a board, your best
sneakers, new box of panty liners turned hall bathroom
into padded cell
"Hey Mama, you angry? Wanna watch me River Dance?"
And there you go,
hoofing your way out of trouble,
while mending my heart.
— **Kelly Clayton, poet, "Mr. Fixit"**

[Motherhood] toughens you up and makes you more pragmatic, yet at the same time it turns you into a bowl of mush. You see a child in distress or a puppy waiting to cross the street and you just want to weep.

—*Cate Blanchett, actor*

Parenthood is shit, snot, slime, fear, tears, spit, and spills. It's as intense as combat, which is to say hours of tedium relieved by moments of alarm and flashes of joy to remind you that you're alive.

—*Scott Simon, journalist*

There is nothing that can bring you closer to fearlessness about everything else in the world than being a parent— because everyday fears—like not being approved of—pale by comparison to the fears you have about your children.

—*Arianna Huffington, columnist and media group editor-in-chief*

It takes courage to raise children.

—*John Steinbeck, novelist*

You have to be strong and in charge of yourself to raise someone else.

—*Donna Summer, singer-songwriter*

They say that man is mighty,
He governs land and sea,
He wields a mighty scepter
O'er lesser powers that be;
But a mightier power and stronger
Man from his throne has hurled,
For the hand that rocks the cradle
Is the hand that rules the world.
—William Ross Wallace, poet,
from "What Rules the World"

I saw a stony mask come upon her lined face as she slew the weak housewife she had been and gave birth to the warrior that is buried inside every woman's heart, one who is unleashed when her children's lives are at stake.

—*Kamran Pasha, writer and producer*

Sometimes being a good mother gets in the way of being a good person.

—Elizabeth Forsythe Hailey, journalist

Do your thing and don't care if they like it.

—*Tina Fey, actor and comedian*

The child of a tiger is a tiger.

—*Haitian proverb*

Hell has no fury like a woman scorned, but a woman scorned has nothing on a mother protecting her young.

—*Richard Kevin Hartley, writer*

Maybe, like my parents and grandparents, I can trust myself to be a mom without a reference library to tell me how. Maybe I don't need magazines, television or the Internet to tell me how. And maybe most of all I don't need marketing campaigns designed to make money off my good intentions to tell me how. Maybe I know how.
Or, by God, I'll figure it out.

—*Muffy Mead-Ferro, writer*

If there must be trouble, let it be in my day so my child may have peace.

—*Thomas Paine, writer, radical, and inventor*

Do not believe in anything simply because you have heard it. Do not believe in anything simply because it is spoken and rumored by many. Do not believe in anything simply because it is found written in your religious books. Do not believe in anything merely on the authority of your teachers and elders. Do not believe in traditions because they have been handed down for many generations. But after observation and analysis, when you find that anything agrees with reason and is conducive to the good and benefit of one and all, then accept it and live up to it.

—*Buddha, spiritual teacher*

In spite of the six thousand manuals on childraising in the bookstores, childraising is still a dark continent and no one really knows anything. You just need a lot of love and luck—and, of course, courage.

—*Bill Cosby, comedian, actor, and educator*

Trust yourself. You know more than you think you do.

—*Benjamin Spock, pediatrician*

The selfishness that a woman has learned to stifle or to dissemble where she alone is concerned, blooms freely and unashamed on behalf of her offspring.

—Emily James Putnam, educator and historian

The mother . . . swinging the children by pulling on a length of string, while at the same time she kept an eye on them with that protective watchfulness, half animal, half angelic, which is the quality of motherhood.

—*Victor Hugo, writer and activist*

There's no bitch on earth like a mother frightened for her kids.

—*Stephen King, novelist*

One of the greatest challenges I've faced as a mother—especially in these anxious, winner-takes-all times—is the need to resist the urge to accept someone else's definition of success and to try to figure out, instead, what really is best for my own children, what unique combination of structure and freedom, nurturing and challenge, education and exploration, each of them needs in order to grow and bloom.

—*Katrina Kenison, editor and writer*

Lord, give to men who are old and rougher
The things that little children suffer,
And let keep bright and undefiled
The young years of the little child.
—John Masefield, poet laureate, from "Everlasting Mercy"

She made me a security blanket when I was born. That faded green blanket lasted just long enough for me to realize that the security part came from her.

—Alexander Crane, writer

Motherhood brings out your most animal instinct.

—*Kate Beckinsale, actor*

While the mother sleeps, her toes are awake.

—Creole proverb

If you hate your lot but wouldn't trade it, it's not your lot you hate.

—Mignon McLaughlin, journalist

Mama took me in her arms and held me tight. Her embrace was hot and she smelled like sweat, dust, and grease, but I wanted her. I wanted to crawl inside her mind to find that place that let her smile and sing through the worst dust storms. If I had to be crazy, I wanted my mama's kind of crazy, because she was never afraid.

—*Sarah Zettel, novelist*

She broke the bread into two fragments and gave them to her children, who ate with eagerness. "She hath kept none for herself," grumbled the sergeant. "Because she is not hungry," said a soldier. "No," said the sergeant, "Because she is a mother."

—*Victor Hugo, writer and activist*

I also believe that parents, if they love you, will hold you up safely, above their swirling waters, and sometimes that means you'll never know what they endured, and you may treat them unkindly, in a way you otherwise wouldn't.

—*Mitch Albom, writer, journalist, and broadcaster*

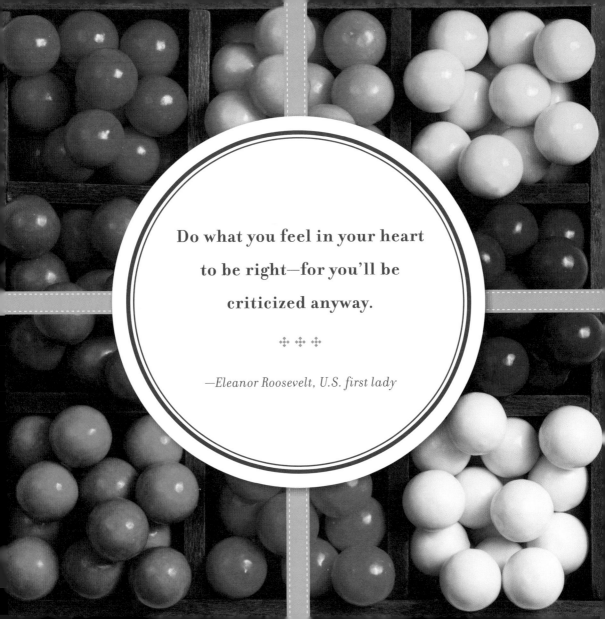

Do what you feel in your heart
to be right—for you'll be
criticized anyway.

✣ ✣ ✣

—*Eleanor Roosevelt, U.S. first lady*

"Can anything harm us, mother, after the night-lights are lit?"
"Nothing, precious," she said; "they are the eyes a mother leaves behind her to guard her children."

—James M. Barrie, novelist

A woman is like a teabag. Only when in hot water do you realize how strong she is.

—Nancy Reagan, U.S. first lady

A little boy and his mother were crossing a river.
Mother: Please hold my hand.
Boy: No Mom, You hold my hand.
Mother: What's the difference?
Boy: If I hold your hand and something happens to me, chances are that I may let your hand go; but if you hold my hand, I know for sure you will never let my hand go.

—Anonymous

When I can remind myself that I am fall-to-my-knees lucky and should be fall-to-my-knees grateful, these big negatives are not so bad as they feel when they first hit.

—*Helen Hunt, actor and director*

Promise me you'll always remember:
You're braver than you believe,
and stronger than you seem,
and smarter than you think.
—**A. A. Milne, writer and playwright**

Let go of perfection. We don't always have the answers, the energy, and the foresight to control everything that happens in parenthood. She who doesn't bend, snaps. The key to mothering is malleability. Stretching, expanding, widening, deepening. When we surrender perfection we become more tolerant of ourselves and others. We invite surprise. We relax about the small things. We're more forgiving and more open-minded. We adapt to change, and even enjoy it sometimes. We become more forgiving of others—and, most importantly, ourselves. When we're flexible, change, the only constant in parenting, is less shocking. Motherhood defies and redefines perfection.

We have a family mantra, you know, "Why do it right when you can do it yourself?"

—*Uma Thurman, actor*

Trust your own instinct. Your mistakes might as well be your own, instead of someone else's.

—*Billy Wilder, filmmaker*

If everything is under control, you're going too slow.

—*Mario Andretti, race car driver*

Life is to be lived, not controlled.

—*Ralph Ellison, novelist*

I'd like to be the ideal mother, but I'm too busy raising my kids.

—*Anonymous*

I've let a lot of my type A personality go. When you have a kid, the messiness doesn't matter anymore.

—Tiffani Thiessen, actor

It's a marathon; it's not a sprint.

—Melinda Gates, philanthropist

Being a parent forces us to accept and live with imperfection. We work with our kids to overcome their challenges. Being a parent reminds us that our co-workers were children once, that they had their own struggles, that their childhood experiences helped them become the person, they are today. That kind of tolerance and acceptance doesn't have to be left at home . . . it can benefit everyone.

—Sheryl Sandberg, chief operating officer, Facebook

Have no fear of perfection—you'll never reach it.

—Salvador Dalí, artist

I have to not try and think that everything has to be 100% perfect all the time and leave room for error. As long as my kids feel loved and a priority, everything really is secondary.

—*Jessica Alba, actor*

The brain actually does the opposite of what you expect when you are a perfectionist—it slows down to make sure rather than speeding up. And life then becomes harder than you imagine because you are constantly striving to slow down to hit the mark rather than living in the flow.

—*Srini Pillay, medical doctor*

No one ever died from sleeping in an unmade bed. I have known mothers who remake the bed after their children do it because there's a wrinkle in the spread or the blanket is on crooked. This is sick.

—*Erma Bombeck, writer and humorist*

I think that the biggest lesson in being a mom is that there are so many things that you can't control. God has entrusted me with this little life. I can certainly make sure he eats fruits and vegetables, but there is a whole lot that I cannot direct and guide as he grows, matures.

—*Nichole Nordeman, singer-songwriter*

Parenting isn't a noun but a verb—an ongoing process instead of an accomplishment.

—*Jodi Picoult, novelist*

Out beyond ideas of wrong-doing and right-doing, there is a field. I'll meet you there.

—*Rumi, poet*

"Done" is better than "perfect."

—*American proverb*

If you can control your behavior
when everything around you is out of control,
you can model for your children a valuable
lesson in patience and understanding . . . and
snatch an opportunity to shape character.

—Jane Clayson Johnson, writer and journalist

When you surrender, the problem ceases to
exist. Try to solve it, or conquer it, and you only
set up more resistance. . . . The most difficult
thing to admit, and to realize with one's whole
being, is that you alone control nothing.

— Henry Miller, writer and painter

Even if I'm setting myself up for failure, I think it's worth trying to be a mother who delights in who her children are, in their knock-knock jokes and earnest questions. A mother who spends less time obsessing about what will happen, or what has happened, and more time reveling in what is. . . . A mother who doesn't worry so much about being bad or good but just recognizes that she's both, and neither.

—*Ayelet Waldman, lawyer and writer*

I was a wonderful parent before I had children.

—*Adele Faber, writer*

. . . Trying to be a good mother may be as distant from being a good one as trying to have a good time is from truly having one.

—*Lionel Shriver, novelist*

Striving to better, oft we mar what's well.

—*William Shakespeare, playwright*

Very early in our children's lives we will be forced to realize that the "perfect" untroubled life we'd like for them is just a fantasy. In daily living, tears and fights and doing things we don't want them to do are all part of our human ways of developing into adult.

—*Fred Rogers, television personality*

You may not control all the events that happen to you, but you can decide not to be reduced by them.

—*Maya Angelou, poet and novelist*

It will help us and our children if we can laugh at our faults. It will help us tolerate our shortcomings, and it will help our children see that the goal is to be human, not perfect.

—*Neil Kurshan, rabbi*

Don't try to be perfect; just be an excellent example of being human.

—Anthony Robbins, motivational speaker

When you say or do anything to please, get, keep, influence, or control anyone or anything, fear is the cause and pain is the result.

—Byron Katie, writer and inspirational speaker

Some things in life are out of your control. You can make it a party or a tragedy.

—Nora Roberts, novelist

Wear a bright red shirt with bright orange shorts? Sure. Put water in the toy tea set? Okay. Sleep with your head at the foot of the bed? Fine. Samuel Johnson said, "All severity that does not tend to increase good, or prevent evil, is idle."

—Gretchen Rubin, writer and attorney

The vow that binds too strictly snaps itself.

—*Alfred, Lord Tennyson, poet and Nobel Laureate*

Anybody out there who is a parent, if your kids want to paint their bedrooms, as a favor to me, let them do it. It'll be OK.

—*Randy Pausch, computer scientist and writer*

If we can just let go and trust that things will work out the way they're supposed to, without trying to control the outcome, then we can begin to enjoy the moment more fully. The joy of the freedom it brings becomes more pleasurable than the experience itself.

—*Goldie Hawn, actor*

God grant me the serenity
To accept the things I cannot change;
the courage to change the things I can;
and the wisdom to know the difference.
—*Reinhold Niebuhr, poet, "Serenity Prayer"*

Did your mom ever tell you, "If you can't say something nice, don't say anything?" She was right—and talking nicely also applies when you're talking to yourself, even inside your head.

—*Victoria Moran, writer and spiritual teacher*

If babies held the same tendency toward self-criticism as adults, they might never learn to walk or talk. Can you imagine infants stomping, "Aarggh! Screwed up again!" Fortunately, babies are free of self-criticism. They just keep practicing.

—*Dan Millman, athlete*

Every day I try, and often fail, to be the mother who doesn't mess up! But no matter what, [my son] knows that I love him. And I know that bedrock of unconditional love is a child's most important foundation.

—*Christiane Amanpour, television news anchor*

To me, the defining trait of working mothers is flexibility.

—*Judsen Culbreth, publishing executive*

Once you accept the fact that you're not perfect, then you develop some confidence.

—*Rosalynn Carter, U.S. first lady*

Mothers are only human...You turn it over to God and then you just wing it.

—*Jo-Ann Mapson, novelist*

They say that parenting is like dancing. You take one step, your child takes another.

—*Michael Jackson, singer, artist, and entertainer*

For me, the answer lies in facing one's perceived deficiencies head-on. I know that I'm prone to depression. That I need far too much sleep. That I need a lot of me-time and solitude. That I swear far too often in front of little ears and buy too many handbags. I also know that I love my children madly, truly, deeply, and that I will always do the best for them that I can. And that is what keeps me afloat.

—*Jen Lawrence, writer*

It's frightening to think that you mark your children merely by being yourself. . . . It seems unfair. You can't assume the responsibility for everything you do—or don't do.

—*Simone de Beauvoir, novelist*

The only person who never makes mistakes is the person who never does anything.

—*Denis Waitley, motivational speaker*

God knows that a mother needs fortitude and courage and tolerance and flexibility and patience and firmness and nearly every other brave aspect of the human soul. But because I happen to be a parent of almost fiercely maternal nature, I praise casualness. It seems to me the rarest of virtues. It is useful enough when children are small. It is useful to the point of necessity when they are adolescents.

—Phyllis McGinley, poet and children's writer

The only thing we can do is play on the one string we have, and that is our attitude. . . . I am convinced that life is 10% what happens to me and 90% how I react to it. And so it is with you . . . we are in charge of our attitudes.

—Charles R. Swindoll, pastor and educator

Everybody says women are like water. I think it's because water is the source of life, and it adapts itself to its environment. Like women, water also gives of itself wherever it goes to nurture life.

—Xue Xinran, journalist

Good judgment comes from experience, and experience comes from bad judgment.

—*Rita Mae Brown, novelist and screenwriter*

Rest easy, real mothers. The very fact that you worry about being a good mom means that you already are one.

—*Jodi Picoult, novelist*

Living the basic good-mothering guidelines enables a mom to blend the responsibilities of parenthood with its joys; to know when to stand her ground and when to be flexible; and to absorb the lessons of the parenting gurus while also trusting her inner voice when it reasons that another cookie isn't worth fighting over, or that her child won't suffer irreparable trauma if, once in awhile, Mom puts her own needs first.

—*Sue Woodman, journalist and broadcaster*

Flexibility makes buildings to be stronger, imagine what it can do to your soul.

—*Carlos Barrios, priest and anthropologist*

It's so hard. I just say, give yourself a break 'cause it's really hard. And don't believe it when you think other people are making a success of it and it's all smooth and easy 'cause it isn't. You know . . . there's never enough of you to go around.

—*Emily Watson, actor*

All life is an experiment. The more experiments you make, the better.

—*Ralph Waldo Emerson, essayist and poet*

Parents should sit tall in the saddle and look upon their troops with a noble and benevolent and extremely nearsighted gaze.

—*Garrison Keillor, storyteller, humorist, and radio personality*

YOU'VE GOT TO JUMP OFF CLIFFS ALL THE TIME AND BUILD YOUR WINGS ON THE WAY DOWN.

—ANNIE DILLARD, NOVELIST

The human capacity for burden is like bamboo—far more flexible than you'd ever believe at first glance.

—Jodi Picoult, *novelist*

That which yields is not always weak.

—Jacqueline Carey, *novelist*

The strongest steel is forged by the fires of hell. It is pounded and struck repeatedly before it's plunged back into the molten fire. The fire gives it power and flexibility, and the blows give it strength.

—Sherrilyn Kenyon, *novelist*

I know why families were created with all their imperfections. They humanize you. They are made to make you forget yourself occasionally, so that the beautiful balance of life is not destroyed.

—*Anaïs Nin, novelist*

Hold fast to whatever fragments of love that exist, for sometimes a mosaic is more beautiful than an unbroken pattern.

—Dawn Powell, novelist

No relationship is perfect, ever. There are always some ways you have to bend, to compromise, to give something up in order to gain something greater. . . . Love can make up for a lot.
—Sarah Dessen, novelist

You don't tolerate parenthood. You don't survive it. You grow with it.

—Michael Baron, novelist

[Motherhood is] a constant dance with faith, one step toward the unknown and two steps back to the familiar.
—Lisa Groen Braner, writer

Mothering is really about change. It is how we adapt to change that will make a difference in helping our children grow up.

—Debby Russell, writer

Life is a series of natural and spontaneous changes. Don't resist them; that only creates sorrow. Let reality be reality. Let things flow naturally forward in whatever way they like.

—*Lao Tzo, philosopher*

Good mothers know that their relationship with each of their children is like a movable feast, constantly changing and evolving.

—*Sue Woodman, journalist and broadcaster*

Learn to adapt. Things change, circumstances change. Adjust yourself and your efforts to what it is presented to you so you can respond accordingly. Never see change as a threat, because it can be an opportunity to learn, to grow, evolve and become a better person.

—*Rodolfo Costa, writer*

To be ourselves while remaining adaptable, we must either justify a decision to change as being consistent with our identity, or we must acknowledge that our identity itself is malleable but no less authentic for it. The challenge is to feel that although we have not always been exactly who we are now, we will nevertheless always recognize ourselves.

—*Sheena Iyengar, professor*

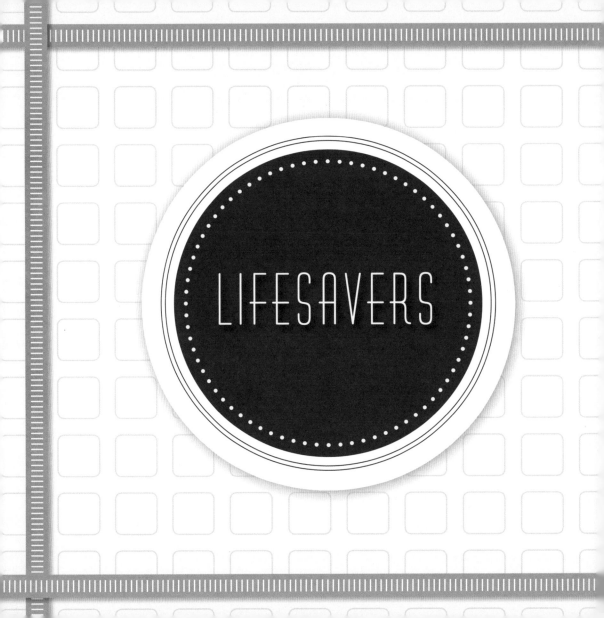

We're over our heads half the time. What keeps us afloat? Lifesavers—partners, friends, family, and any others who are there to support you. Frazzled is the mother who thinks she can do it all by herself. We need other people to laugh with and lean on. Every mother needs a support system—not because she can't do it alone, but because it's so difficult. Recall the survival instruction given on airplanes: Put your own oxygen mask on first, and then do the same for others. There's logic to this. If you can't breathe easily, no one else can either.

The hand that rocks the cradle usually is attached to someone who isn't getting enough sleep.

—John Fiebig, writer

You can make it, but it's easier if you don't have to do it alone.

—Betty Ford, U.S. first lady

What gets me through the hard days? Other moms, especially mine, and friends and even total strangers at the park who laugh with me about the hilarious business of raising a child.

—Carol Lin, news anchor

When you're drowning, you don't say, "I would be incredibly pleased if someone would have the foresight to notice me drowning and come and help me." You just scream.

—John Lennon, musician and singer-songwriter

Don't be afraid to ask for help. You should try to get help wherever you can. Don't guilt yourself, it doesn't help. Do anything you can to try to save time with the dumb stuff around the house so you can be with your kids as much as you can.

—Jennifer Garner, actor

Don't be shy about asking for help. It doesn't mean you're weak, it only means you're wise.

—Anonymous

I believe we do all have the biological hard-wiring for a parenting instinct, and this instinct comes through in flying colours when we feel well supported and nurtured by our families and communities.

—Robin Grille, psychologist

Being a mother is not a matter of running through a succession of chores.

—Naomi Stadlen, writer and psychotherapist

The great motherhood friendships
are the ones in which two women
can admit [how difficult mothering
is] quietly to each other, over
cups of tea at a table sticky with
spilled apple juice and littered with
markers without tops.

—*Anna Quindlen, journalist and novelist*

Refusing to ask for help when you need it is refusing someone the chance to be helpful.

—Ric Ocasek, musician

Sometimes you just need a minute to say, "I think I'm cracking" and just acknowledge it.

—Tina Fey, actor and comedian

I think there is sometimes too much pressure on us to be perfect parents, to be empathetic and loving all the time. Every woman needs a good girlfriend to be able to turn to and say, "I just can't deal with it all today."

—Rachel Weisz, actor and model

Friends are like bras: close to your heart and there for support.

—Anonymous

You were never meant to live on Planet Mom alone and disconnected. You were meant to have relationships filled with joy and depth and meaning—something you want to model for young children.

—*Lisa Bergren, novelist*

Oh, the comfort—the inexpressible comfort of feeling safe with a person—having neither to weigh thoughts nor measure words, but pouring them all right out, just as they are, chaff and grain together; certain that a faithful hand will take and sift them, keep what is worth keeping, and then with the breath of kindness blow the rest away.

—*Dinah Maria Mulock Craik, novelist*

Friendship is a sheltering tree.

—*Samuel Taylor Coleridge, poet*

That was the thing about best friends. Like sisters and mothers, they could piss you off and make you cry and break your heart, but in the end, when the chips were down, they were there, making you laugh even in your darkest hours.

—*Kristin Hannah, novelist*

Parenthood: The state of being better chaperoned than you were before marriage.

—*Marcelene Cox, writer*

Behind me, on one bank, is the tribe of women who are not mothers. They drink coffee, stay up late, skip meals, plan careers, change lovers, study Sanskrit, and write grant proposals for a five-year study of tropical cloud forests. In front of me, on the other bank, is the tribe of mothers. They arrive late, leave early, are badly in need of haircuts, talk a lot about nap schedules, know way too much about guinea pigs, and have to hang up now.

—*Sandra Steingraber, biologist and speaker*

Give me other
mothers and
I will give you
another world.

—*Saint Augustine,
philosopher and
theologian*

Only surround
yourself with
people who will lift
you higher.

—*Oprah Winfrey, talk
show host, actor, and
philanthropist*

One day you will do things for me
that you hate. That is what it means
to be family.

—*Jonathan Safran Foer, novelist*

Eventually you can get into the nuts and bolts of reality: nurturing, caring, and getting along.

—Jody Watley, singer-songwriter

Women without children are also the best of mothers, often, with the patience, interest, and saving grace that the constant relationship with children cannot always sustain. . . . Women who are not mothering their own children have the clarity and focus to see deeply into the character of children webbed by family. A child is fortunate who feels witnessed as a person, outside relationships with parents by another adult.

—Louise Erdrich, novelist

Friendship makes prosperity brighter, while it lightens adversity by sharing its griefs and anxieties.

—Cicero, philosopher and orator

Friendship is born at that moment when one person says to another, "What! You too? I thought I was the only one."
—*C. S. Lewis, novelist, scholar, and poet*

We need to feel like there's a little bit of fun left in us. For example, one of my girlfriends might come over after I put Isabel to bed, and we'll eat cookie dough and have a glass of wine each—just one glass—we're responsible! But you're still a woman, you're still a friend, and you still want to hear a good piece of gossip from the neighborhood—none of that changes.
—*Angela Kinsey, actor*

I don't care about whose DNA has recombined with whose. When everything goes to hell, the people who stand by you without flinching—they are your family.
—*Jim Butcher, novelist*

Babies don't need fathers, but mothers do. Someone who is taking care of a baby needs to be taken care of.

—Amy Heckerling, film director

It is important for a husband to understand that his words have tremendous power in his wife's life. He needs to bless her with words. She's given her life to love and care for him, to partner with him, to create a family together, to nurture his children. . . . Every single day, a husband should tell his wife, "I love you. I appreciate you. You're the best thing that ever happened to me."

—Joel Osteen, pastor

The most important thing a father can do for his children is to love their mother.

—Theodore Hesburgh, priest

When Dad can't get the diaper straight we laugh at him as though he were trying to walk around in high-heeled shoes. Do we ever point out that all you have to do is lay out the diaper like a baseball diamond, put the kid's butt on the pitcher's mound, bring home plate up, then fasten the tapes at first and third base?

—**Michael Meyerhoff**, *parent educator*

Romance has shifted a lot since we had kids. It sometimes means allowing your partner the space to be alone, sleep late, or go out with friends while the other handles bedtime solo. That's a far cry from sexy lingerie, rose petals in a bathtub, or a fancy French dinner with a good game of footsie, but once we had kids, we started to realize that what often ignites passion for each other is when my husband or I shows compassion and understanding of our stresses and struggles to stay sane amid chaos.

—*Mayim Bialik, actor and neuroscientist*

Your kids are happy if you're happy. And if your love is happy, then everything works. I think a lot of people think once the children are there, it's all about the children. But you can't forget about your best friend, your lover, your husband.

—*Heidi Klum, model and fashion designer*

My breakthrough moment was when I convinced my husband that when the toddler woke up in the middle of the night and screamed, "Mommy," he actually meant, "Parent of either sex."

—*Sallie Krawcheck, former president of Bank of America*

There is nothing to indicate any biological need for an exclusive primary bond; nothing to suggest that mothering cannot be shared by several people.

—*H. R. Schaffer, psychologist*

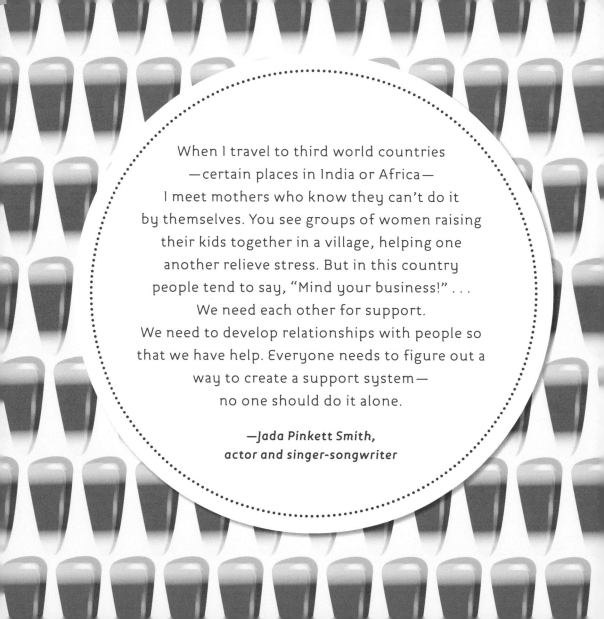

When I travel to third world countries
—certain places in India or Africa—
I meet mothers who know they can't do it
by themselves. You see groups of women raising
their kids together in a village, helping one
another relieve stress. But in this country
people tend to say, "Mind your business!" . . .
We need each other for support.
We need to develop relationships with people so
that we have help. Everyone needs to figure out a
way to create a support system—
no one should do it alone.

—Jada Pinkett Smith,
actor and singer-songwriter

Nobody has ever before asked the nuclear family to live all by itself in a box the way we do. With no relatives, no support, we've put it in an impossible situation.

—Margaret Mead, anthropologist

When a couple has an argument nowadays they may think it is about money or power or sex or how to raise the kids or whatever. What they're really saying to each other, though without realizing it, is this: "You are not enough people!"

—Kurt Vonnegut Jr., novelist

Accept offers of help! . . . My mother used to take my kids every Sunday morning, a blessed time during which I'd go to the gym and do my shopping. It was heaven, and she also forged a strong relationship with her grandkids during that time. Yes, she may have done things differently with my kids than I would have. So what? Who cares? It's good for kids to be exposed to different ideas.

—Lisa Bloom, attorney and journalist

They say "LOVE" is an acronym for "Let Other Versions Exist!"
— *Nancy Pelosi, speaker of the U.S. House of Representatives*

I like to hire people who tell me they can take on more. After I became a mother, I upped the definition of more.
—*Carolyn Kepcher, executive vice president, The Trump Organization*

Sometimes we need help from a god.

—*Tina Turner, singer and actor*

Wrong brand of dish soap bought when someone helps with the shopping? No big deal. Laundry not folded in perfect quartiles? Who cares? Children fed ketchup and crackers for dinner by well-meaning grandparents? Thank the person profusely and go forward. What we lose in control . . . we more than gain in letting others lighten our load.
—*Bethany Casarjian and Diane Dillon, psychologists*

Multiple caregivers enhance the cognitive skills of babies and young children. Any family in which there are parents, grandparents, nannies and other concerned adults understands how readily children adapt to different caregivers. Surely this prepares them better for life than stressed-out biological parents alone.

—Erica Jong, novelist

Other people—grandparents, sisters and brothers, the mother's best friend, the next-door neighbor—get to be familiar to the baby. If the mother communicates her trust in these people, the baby will regard them as delicious novelties. Anybody the mother trusts whom the baby sees often enough partakes a bit of the presence of the mother.

—Louise J. Kaplan, psychoanalyst and scholar

Your empathy for other mothers is such a natural instinct and it's such a beautiful thing that we all connect, and we should all help each other. We should all help each other.

—Salma Hayek, actor

You have this empathy suddenly—this compassion for a mother going through anything complicated or difficult with a child. It's something that I understand now—that unbelievable drive and instinct to protect.

—*Katherine Heigl, actor*

At its best motherhood is a communal project. It takes a village, sometimes several villages, indeed.

—Edwidge Danticat, novelist

The origin of love for fellow humans lies in the mother.

—Kongo proverb

Motherhood has taught me to be more connected to other human beings. All mothers everywhere, we are all responsible for each other. . . . So if you're fighting a battle alone, choose not to fight it alone.

—Sophie Trudeau, musician

We are all travelers in the
wilderness of this world, and
the best we can find in our
travels is an honest friend.

✢ ✢ ✢

—Robert Louis Stevenson,
novelist and poet

My daughter is every mother's child and every mother is the mother of my child.

—*Glenn Close, actor*

One quiet day when we have grown old, we will realize we are not the same person we once were, because once you learn to truly love one human being completely, loving everybody else comes so much easier.

—*Janene Wolsey Baadsgaard, journalist and speaker*

We are, most of us, ready to explode, especially when our children are small and we are so weary with the demands for love and attention and the kind of service that makes you feel you should be wearing a uniform with "Mommy" embroidered over the left breast, over the heart. . . . If a stranger had come up to me and said, "Do you want to talk about it? I have time to listen," I think I might have burst into tears at the relief of it.

—*Elizabeth Berg, novelist*

Le Guin's Rule: One person cannot do two full-time jobs,
but two persons can do three full-time jobs.

—*Ursula K. Le Guin, novelist*

Call it a clan, call it a network, call it a tribe, call it a family:
Whatever you call it, whoever you are, you need one.

—*Jane Howard, novelist*

RENEWAL

Because no mother is an island, we need to retreat to one from time to time. That is, we all need a refuge—a world separate and apart from being a mother where we may replenish our spirits. How to renew? Refilling the cup may mean an emptying of the mind. It's an extra hour of beauty sleep, a random meander in the middle of the day. It's gossip, pillow talk, the luxury of losing ourselves in a novel. It's a moment of grace, eyes closed and breathing deeply. It's whatever we do to restore and refuel. Most of all, renewal means taking care of ourselves. For how can we take care of our children if we don't?

There was never a child so lovely, but his mother was glad to get him to sleep.

—*Ralph Waldo Emerson, essayist and poet*

The joys of motherhood are never fully experienced until the children are in bed.

—*Anonymous*

How beautiful it is to do nothing, and then rest afterward.

—*Spanish proverb*

Love can be unselfish, in the sense of being benevolent and generous, without being selfless.

—*Mortimer Adler, philosopher and educator*

Self-love, my liege, is not so vile a sin, as self-neglecting.

—*William Shakespeare, playwright*

I love my family, my children ... but inside myself is a place where I live all alone and that's where you renew your springs that never dry up.

—Pearl S. Buck, novelist

Over and over again, her own direct experience teaches a woman that when she does enough for herself, she feels better and better about her child.

—Roger Gould, psychotherapist

We say our families are our priorities, but oftentimes we forget we're members of that family too. If we don't take care of our health, we're not going to be any good to anybody.

—Kathy Ireland, model and businesswoman

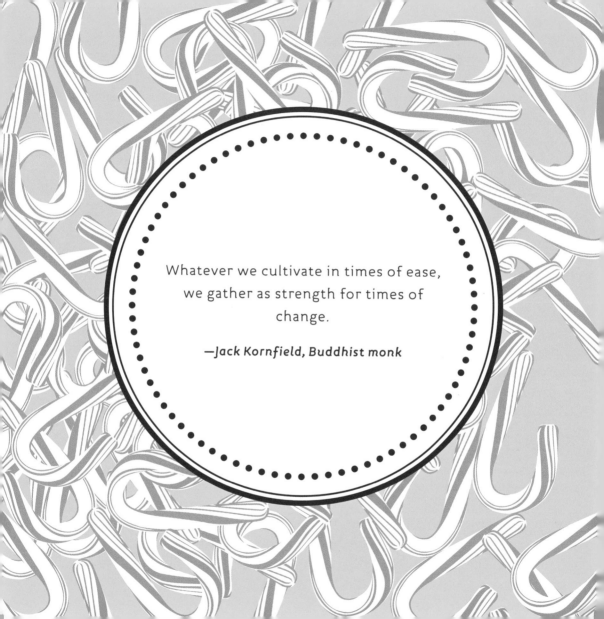

Whatever we cultivate in times of ease, we gather as strength for times of change.

—*Jack Kornfield, Buddhist monk*

Sometimes I get up very early in the morning and enjoy a quiet house and cup of tea before the craziness begins. Other times, I'll take a quick walk on the beach. You can find peace in a few minutes.

—Cindy Crawford, model

I learned that to court a muse, one needs musing time; and that for a mother, this does not necessarily mean thinking, so much as it means emptying the head [of trivia and daily concerns].

—Robyn Sarah, poet

Mother's room and mother's need for privacy become a valuable lesson in respect for other people's rights.

—Doris Lessing, novelist

It's important to be heroic, ambitious, productive, efficient, creative, and progressive, but these qualities don't necessarily nurture soul. The soul has different concerns, of equal value: downtime for reflection, conversation, and reverie; beauty that is captivating and pleasuring; relatedness to the environs and to people; and any animal's rhythm of rest and activity.

—*Thomas Moore, poet and singer-songwriter*

You have to put on your own oxygen mask before you put on others. . . . It's a good metaphor for parenting,.....

—*Amanda Peet, actor*

The children understand that when I have the [beauty] mask on, it's mummy time—it's the working mother's best friend, because you may be exhausted, but you don't want people to know.

—*Cate Blanchett, actor*

Take care of yourself. If Mommy isn't happy, no one else in the family is happy either.

—*Debra Gilbert Rosenberg, psychotherapist*

If you don't give to yourself, but you are giving to everybody else, that you turn around, and you recognize but "I have nobody to give to anymore, and I haven't nurtured myself while I've been nurturing everybody else."

—*Tori Amos, singer-songwriter*

Advice for the day: If you have a headache, do what it says on the aspirin bottle: Take two, and KEEP AWAY FROM CHILDREN.

—*Anonymous*

The quickest way for a parent to get a child's attention is to sit down and look comfortable.

—*Lane Olinghouse, writer*

Go to the bathroom. It's the only place in the house that's quiet.

—*Sarah Maizes, writer*

Children can't be a center of life and a reason for being. They can be a thousand satisfying things that are delightful, interesting, satisfying, but they can't be a wellspring to live from. Or they shouldn't be.

—*Doris Lessing, novelist*

Until mothers make peace with who they are, they'll never be content with what they have.

—*Doris Mortman, novelist*

You need to remember the best legacy you can give your kids is an example of a life well lived. They may listen to what you say, but they will do what you do. If you tell them to take care of yourself but you don't do it yourself, what kind of message are you sending?

—*Brooke Castillo, life coach*

When a woman becomes her own
best friend, life is easier.

—Diane von Furstenberg,
fashion designer

If you don't think about sex during those first months when you are so meshed with your baby, you wake up six years later not a woman, but a mom. Being sexual and being a person with a strong sense of who she is are ideas that are very tied together.

—*Nancy Friday, writer*

[G]iving yourself some loving attention is not selfish. It is sensible. If you feel loved and cherished—even if it is only by yourself—then you will have more love to give to others, too.

—*Penelope Quest, spiritual teacher*

We can't nourish our children if we don't nourish ourselves. . . . Parents who manage to stay married, sane, and connected to each other share one basic characteristic: the ability to protect even small amounts of time together no matter what else is going on in their lives.

—*Ron Taffel, psychologist*

Home is the one place in all this world where hearts are sure of each other. It is the place of confidence. It is the place where we tear off that mask of guarded and suspicious coldness which the world forces us to wear in self-defense, and where we pour out the unreserved communications of full and confiding hearts. It is the spot where expressions of tenderness gush out without any sensation of awkwardness and without any dread of ridicule.

—**Frederick W. Robertson, divine**

To put the world right in order, we must first put the
nation in order;
to put the nation in order, we must first put the
family in order;
to put the family in order, we must first cultivate
our personal life;
we must first set our hearts right.
—Confucius, philosopher

We want our kids to stand on their own two feet, and we tell them to think for themselves. From their first steps, we root for their independence. Why, then, is it so hard to let them go? Bittersweet is the reality that children grow up, up, and away. What mother hasn't looked back at her child's old clothes and toys without a twinge of sadness? Who doesn't get sentimental about the last of all the first times and the beginning of all the last times? The fond memories we keep, but the kid we must release. Allowing children to become increasingly independent is an act of trust, respect—and love. First they walk; then they fly.

There are only two lasting bequests we can hope to give our children. One of these is roots; the other, wings.

—Hodding Carter, journalist

It kills you to see them grow up. But I guess it would kill you quicker if they didn't.

—Barbara Kingsolver, novelist and poet

You know children are growing up when they start asking questions that have answers.

—John Plomp, writer

The natural term of the affection of the human animal for its offspring is six years.

—George Bernard Shaw, playwright and Nobel Laureate

Mother Nature is providential. She gives us twelve years to develop a love for our children before turning them into teenagers.

—William Galvin, politician

Adolescence is like cactus.

—Anaïs Nin, novelist

Oh, to be half as wonderful as my child thought I was when he was small, and only half as stupid as my teenager now thinks I am.

—Rebecca Richards, writer

It's always been my feeling that God lends you your children until they're about eighteen years old. If you haven't made your points with them by then, it's too late.

—Betty Ford, U.S. first lady

This is part of the essence of motherhood, watching your kid grow into her own person and not being able to do anything about it. Otherwise children would be nothing more than pets.

—Heather Armstrong (Dooce), blogger
and entrepreneur

But kids don't stay with you if you do it right. It's the one job where, the better you are, the more surely you won't be needed in the long run.

—*Barbara Kingsolver, novelist and poet*

One day when she was two years old she was playing in a garden, and she plucked another flower and ran with it to her mother. I suppose she must have looked rather delightful, for Mrs. Darling put her hand to her heart and cried, "Oh, why can't you remain like this forever!" This was all that passed between them on the subject, but henceforth Wendy knew that she must grow up.

—James M. Barrie, novelist

The best way to keep children home is to make the home atmosphere pleasant—and let the air out of the tires.

—Dorothy Parker, writer and satirist

What she did have, after raising two children, was the equivalent of a Ph.D. in mothering and my undying respect.

—Barbara Delinsky, novelist

Ay, these young things lie safe in our hearts just
so long
As their wings are in growing; and when these
are strong
They break it, and farewell! the bird flies!
—*Owen Meredith, statesman and poet, from "Lucile"*

In Mary Oliver's gorgeous poem, "In Blackwater Woods" she explains that to live in this world you must do three things— "to love what is mortal; to hold it against your bones knowing your own life depends on it; and when the time comes to let go, to let it go." My daughter is teaching me every day these lessons of letting go, letting her fall and making her own mistakes, and letting her grow away from me.

—*Andrea Richesin, writer and editor*

Parents rarely let go of their children, so children let go of them. They move on. They move away. The moments that used to define them—a mother's approval, a father's nod—are covered by moments of their own accomplishments. It is not until much later, as the skin sags and the heart weakens, that children understand; their stories, and all their accomplishments, sit atop the stories of their mothers and fathers, stones upon stones, beneath the waters of their lives.

—Mitch Albom, writer, journalist, and broadcaster

Thou, straggler into loving arms
Young climber up of trees
When I forget thy thousand ways,
Then life and all shall cease.
—Mary Lamb, poet, from "A Child"

You transition as a mother
from literally just pulling a booger
out of that person's nose whenever
you see one until at some point
they assert: "No, I'm a person.
You can't fix my underpants
on the subway."

—*Tina Fey, actor and comedian*

The three children grew up and left her as children have a way of doing. She missed them, but it did not end her active life, as her active life had always gone along quite independently of them. . . . It is someday proved to all women that they do not own their children. They were never meant to. And Mrs. Paxton had been wise enough never to pretend she owned her children.

—**F. Scott Fitzgerald, novelist**

The romance of your child's childhood may be the last romance you can give up.

—**Adam Gopnik, writer and commentator**

Kids go where there is excitement. They stay where there is love.

—*Zig Ziglar, motivational speaker*

Imagine a novel in which a woman took in a stranger who was unable to walk or talk or even eat by himself. She fell completely in love with him at first sight, fed and clothed and washed him, and gradually helped him to become more competent and independent, spent more than half her income on him, nursed him through sickness, and thought about him more than anything else. And after about twenty years of this she helped him find a young wife and move far away. Caring for children is an awfully fast and efficient way to experience at least a little saintliness.

—*Alison Gopnik, psychologist*

Sometimes the best way to hold on to something is to let it go.

—*Anonymous*

When your children are very young it is impossible to imagine a life where they will not live with you, where you will not see them every day or know what they are doing. As they grow up, you gradually untangle your "self" from their "selves" until the day arrives when you look at your child and realize the role you play in their life is no longer a central one. It's hard to recognize that your child is independent, but it's also incredibly liberating.

—*Maureen Wheeler, publishing entrepreneur*

I would have let him go one finger at a time, until, without his realizing, he'd be floating without me.
And then I thought, perhaps that is what it means to be a [parent]—to teach your child to live without you.

—*Nicole Krauss, novelist*

We have to bide our time and look for the moment of weakness when we can sneak back into their lives and they will see us and remember us for the people who love them unconditionally.

—**Lisa See, novelist**

The last step in parental love involves the release of the beloved; the willing cutting of the cord that would otherwise keep the child in a state of emotional dependence.

—**Lewis Mumford, historian and sociologist**

Don't cry because it's over. Smile because it happened.

—**Theodor Seuss Geisel (Dr. Seuss), writer and cartoonist**

The babe at first feeds upon the mother's bosom, but it is always on her heart.

—**Henry Ward Beecher, clergyman and social reformer**

A mother is a mother from the moment her baby is first placed in her arms until eternity. It didn't matter if her child were three, thirteen, or thirty.

—*Sarah Strohmeyer, novelist*

Grown don't mean nothing to a mother. A child is a child.
They get bigger, older, but grown?
What's that supposed to mean?
In my heart it don't mean a thing.
—*Toni Morrison, novelist and professor*

Children are time capsules that we launch into the future. With what do we hope to fill them? Compassion and dignity. Curiosity and wisdom. The meaning of values, the value of meaning. Love. Health. Sufficient character, creativity, and education to have a good life and be generous with it. An eager desire to better themselves and the world around them. Grace. Confidence. Happiness. Resilience. All that we've taught our children, all that we learned ourselves, can fuel them in the future. That is our legacy. Where will it take them? Far, we hope . . . and also home.

Children are the living messages we send to a time we will not see.

—*Neil Postman, media theorist and critic*

Children are our immortality; in them we see the story of our life written in a fairer hand.

—*Alfred North Whitehead, mathematician and philosopher*

You are the bows from which your children as living arrows are sent forth.

—*Kahlil Gibran, artist and poet*

The oak sleeps in the acorn.

—*James Allen, writer and philosopher*

Only mothers can think of the future—because they give birth to it in their children.

—*Maxim Gorky, writer and activist*

Once you bring life into this world, you must protect it. We must protect it by changing the world.

—*Elie Wiesel, novelist, professor, and political activist*

A hundred years from now it will not matter what my bank account was, the sort of house I lived in, or the kind of car I drove . . . but the world may be different because I was important in the life of a child.

—*Forest E. Witcraft, academic and educator*

The things you do for yourself are gone when you are gone, but the things you do for others remain as your legacy.

—*Kalu Kalu, political scientist*

Many people have said to me "What a pity you had such a big family to raise. Think of the novels and the short stories and the poems you never had time to write because of that." And I looked at my children and I said, "These are my poems. These are my short stories."

—*Olga Masters, journalist and novelist*

I wanted to teach my daughter
the same things I had to unlearn after
years spent as a corporate lawyer:
that soul is more important
than money, that love means
more than material things.

—James Griffioen, *artist*

One generation plants the trees; another gets the shade.

—*Chinese proverb*

A mother has, perhaps, the hardest earthly lot; and yet no mother worthy of the name ever gave herself thoroughly for her child who did not feel that, after all, she reaped what she had sown.

—*Henry Ward Beecher, clergyman and social reformer*

If I have a monument in this world, it is my son.

—*Maya Angelou, poet and novelist*

Let her be sweet because I believe beauty is as beauty does.

—*Halle Berry, actor*

Being a parent wasn't just about bearing a child. It was about bearing witness to its life.

—*Jodi Picoult, novelist*

The human heart was not designed to beat outside the human body and yet, each child represented just that—a parent's heart bared, beating forever outside its chest.

—Debra Ginsberg, novelist

Lead her away from Acting but not all the way to Finance. Something where she can make her own hours but still feel intellectually fulfilled and get outside sometimes.

—Tina Fey, actor and comedian

I would be the most content if my children grew up to be the kind of people who think decorating consists mostly of building enough bookshelves.

—Anna Quindlen, journalist and novelist

We need to let our children grow up to face the world armed with much more knowledge than we ourselves had at that age.
—*Daniel Dennett, cognitive scientist and philosopher*

. . . What I wanted most fervently, was for her to understand that hard work paid off, that decency begat decency, that humility was not a raincoat you occasionally pulled on when you thought conditions called for it, but rather a constant way of existing in the world, knowing that good luck and bad luck touched everyone and none of us was fully responsible for our fortunes or tragedies.

—*Curtis Sittenfeld, novelist*

I want my little girl to tell me who she is so I can encourage her, and not impose my desires for her on her life. I want her to dream big and to know that if she is willing to earn it, she can have anything—and become anything.

—*Salma Hayek, actor*

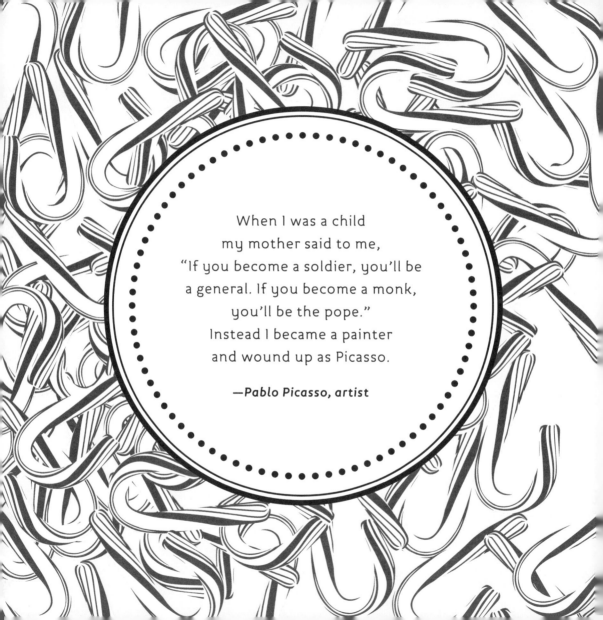

When I was a child
my mother said to me,
"If you become a soldier, you'll be
a general. If you become a monk,
you'll be the pope."
Instead I became a painter
and wound up as Picasso.

—*Pablo Picasso, artist*

The most beautiful sight in the world is a little child going confidently down the road of life after you have shown him the way.

—*Confucius, philosopher*

I don't know what rituals my kids will carry into adulthood, whether they'll grow up attached to homemade pizza on Friday nights, or the scent of peppers roasting over a fire, or what. I do know that flavors work their own ways under the skin, into the heart of longing. Where my kids are concerned I find myself hoping for the simplest things: that if someday they crave orchards where their kids can climb into the branches and steal apples, the world will have trees enough with arms to receive them.

—*Barbara Kingsolver, novelist and poet*

Now I want to make a better world . . . that's motherhood.

—*Cass Elliot, singer*

I want my children to understand the world, but not just because the world is fascinating and the human mind is curious. I want them to understand it so that they will be positioned to make it a better place.

—*Howard Gardner, psychologist*

We must teach our children to dream with their eyes open.

—*Harry Edwards, sociologist*

We don't inherit the Earth from our ancestors, we borrow it from our children.

—*David Brower, environmentalist*

Every mother is like Moses. She does not enter the Promised Land. She prepares a world she will not see.

—*Pope Paul VI, religious leader*

Real generosity toward the future lies in giving all to
the present.

—*Albert Camus, novelist and philosopher*

Child-rearing today was so complicated. You always had to
think of what they'd say on television later.

—*Orson Scott Card, novelist*

**You may not be able to leave your children a great
inheritance, but day by day you may be weaving coats
for them which they will wear through all eternity.**

—*T. L. Cuyler, minister*

Our children are our only hope for the future, but we are their
only hope for their present and their future.

—*Zig Ziglar, motivational speaker*

All of us remember the home of our childhood. Interestingly, our thoughts do not dwell on whether the house was large or small, the neighborhood fashionable or downtrodden. Rather, we delight in the experiences we shared as a family. The home is the laboratory of our lives, and what we learn there largely determines what we do when we leave there.

—*Thomas S. Monson, religious leader*

For nothing is fixed, forever and forever and forever, it is not fixed; the earth is always shifting, the light is always changing, the sea does not cease to grind down rock. Generations do not cease to be born, and we are responsible to them because we are the only witnesses they have. The sea rises, the light fails, lovers cling to each other, and children cling to us. The moment we cease to hold each other, the sea engulfs us and the light goes out.

—*James Baldwin, novelist*

The sacred books of the ancient Persians say, "If you would be holy, instruct your children, because all the good acts they perform will be imputed to you."

—*Montesquieu (Charles-Louis de Secondat), philosopher*

Oh that God would give every mother a vision of the glory
and splendor of the work that is given to her when a babe
is placed in her bosom to be nursed and trained! Could
she have but one glimpse into the future of that life as it
reaches on into eternity; could she look into its soul to see
its possibilities; could she be made to understand her own
personal responsibility for the training of this child, for the
development of its life, and for its destiny, she would see that
in all God's world there is no other work so noble and
so worthy of her best powers, and she would commit to
no others hands the sacred and holy trust given to her.

—J. R. Miller, *writer and pastor*

**Parents are like shuttles on a loom. They join the threads
of the past with threads of the future and leave their own
bright patterns as they go.**

—Fred Rogers, *television personality*

Our children are not going to be just "our children," they are going to be other people's husbands and wives and the parents of our grandchildren.

—*Mary Steichen Calderone, physician and advocate*

Each day of our lives we make deposits in the memory banks of our children.

—*Charles R. Swindoll, pastor and educator*

You have nothing in this world more precious than your children. When you grow old, when your hair turns white and your body grows weary, when you are prone to sit in a rocker and meditate on the things of your life, nothing will be so important as the question of how your children have turned out. It will not be the money you have made. It will not be the cars you have owned. It will not be the large house in which you live. The searing question that will cross your mind again and again will be, *How well have my children done?*

—*Gordon B. Hinckley, religious leader*

Time is the judge. If you manage to pass on what you have to the next generation, then what you did was right.

—*Barbara Kingsolver, novelist and poet*

Mama exhorted her children at every opportunity to "jump at de sun." We might not land on the sun, but at least we would get off the ground.

—*Zora Neale Hurston, anthropologist and novelist*

There were two things about Mama. One is she always expected the best out of me. And the other is that then no matter what I did, whatever I came home with, she acted like it was the moon I had just hung up in the sky and plugged in all the stars. Like I was that good.

—*Barbara Kingsolver, novelist and poet*

My mom is a neverending song in my heart of comfort, happiness, and being. I may sometimes forget the words but I always remember the tune.

—*Graycie Harmon, writer*

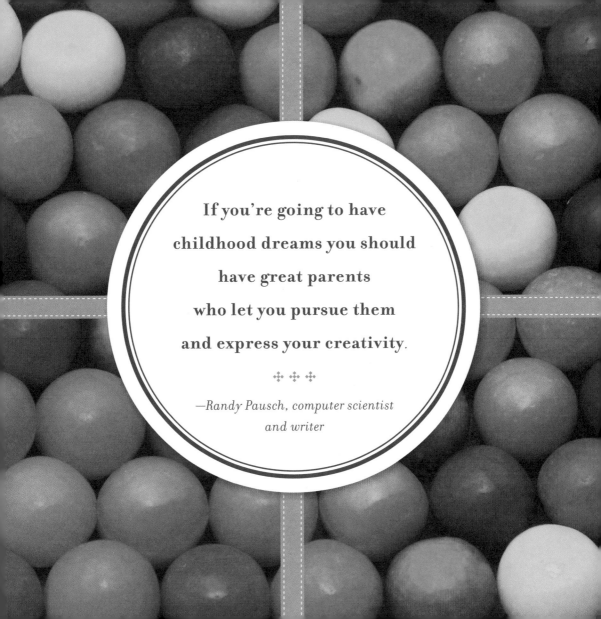

If you're going to have
childhood dreams you should
have great parents
who let you pursue them
and express your creativity.

✤ ✤ ✤

—*Randy Pausch, computer scientist
and writer*

I still hear your humming, Mama. The color of your song calls me home. The color of your words saying, "Let her be. She got a right to be different. She gonna stumble on herself one of these days. Just let the child be."
And I be, Mama.

—*Sonia Sanchez, poet*

I shall never forget my mother, for it was she who planted and nurtured the first seeds of good within me. She opened my heart to the lasting impressions of nature; she awakened my understanding and extended my horizon and her precepts exerted an everlasting influence upon the course of my life.

—*Immanuel Kant, philosopher*

My mother's love for me was so great I have worked hard to justify it.

—*Marc Chagall, artist*

My mother wanted me to be her wings, to fly as she never quite had the courage to do. I love her for that. I love the fact that she wanted to give birth to her own wings.

—*Erica Jong, novelist*

We find these joys to be self-evident: That all children are created whole, endowed with innate intelligence, with dignity and wonder, worthy of respect. The embodiment of life, liberty and happiness, children are original blessings, here to learn their own song. Every girl and boy is entitled to love, to dream and belong to a loving "village." And to pursue a life of purpose.

—*Raffi Cavoukian, singer-songwriter*

Fifty-four years of love and tenderness and crossness and devotion and unswerving loyalty. Without her I could have achieved a quarter of what I have achieved, not only in terms of success and career, but in terms of personal happiness.

—*Noel Coward, playwright and composer*

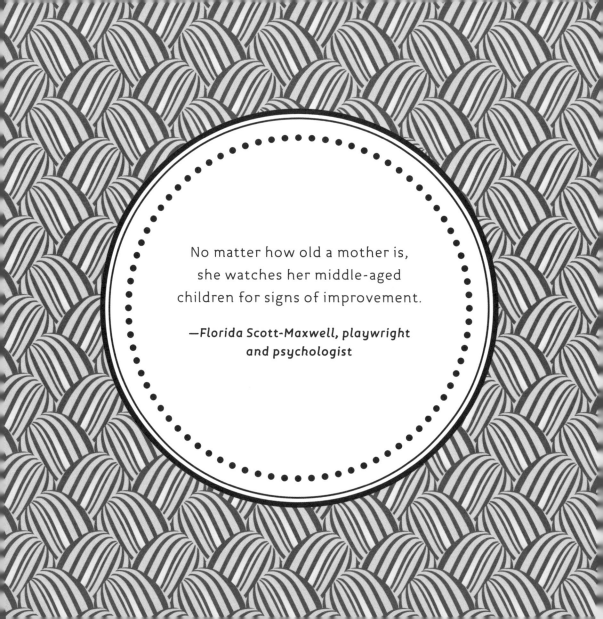

No matter how old a mother is,
she watches her middle-aged
children for signs of improvement.

—*Florida Scott-Maxwell, playwright
and psychologist*

In the man whose childhood has known caresses, there is always a fibre of memory that can be touched to gentle issues.

—*George Eliot, novelist*

My mother was the making of me. She was so true and so sure of me, I felt that I had someone to live for—someone I must not disappoint. The memory of my mother will always be a blessing to me.

—*Thomas A. Edison, inventor and businessman*

If we influence people in a positive way ... even if our social web is only as big as our nuclear family ... others will want to emulate us and pass on our ideas, manners, and lifestyle to future generations. This is more than enough motivation for me to do good things in my life and teach my children to do the same.

—*Greg Graffin, musician and evolutionary biologist*

We may not be able to prepare the future for our children, but we can at least prepare our children for the future.

—Franklin D. Roosevelt, U.S. president

There never was a woman like her. She was gentle as a dove and brave as a lioness. . . . The memory of my mother and her teachings were after all the only capital I had to start life with, and on that capital I have made my way.

—Andrew Jackson, U.S. president

Mama told me to make a special point to remember the best times of my life. There are so many hard things to live through, and latching on to the good things will give you strength to endure.

—Nancy Turner, novelist

My mama used to say, "Are you sad? Then just wait a minute."

—Shannon Hale, novelist

When I stopped seeing my mother with the eyes of a child,
I saw the woman who helped me give birth to myself.

—*Nancy Friday, writer*

Every Mother contains her daughter in herself and every
daughter her mother and every mother extends backwards into
her mother and forwards into her daughter.

—*C. G. Jung, psychiatrist*

And so our mothers and grandmothers have, more often
than not anonymously, handed on the creative spark, the
seed of the flower they themselves never hoped to see—
or like a sealed letter they could not plainly read.

—*Alice Walker, novelist*

[Motherhood] is still the biggest gamble in the world. It is
the glorious life force. It's huge and scary—it's an act of
infinite optimism.

—*Gilda Radner, comedian and actor*

Mama was my greatest teacher,
a teacher of compassion,
love and fearlessness.
If love is sweet as a flower,
then my mother is that sweet
flower of love.

—Stevie Wonder, singer-songwriter

In praising or loving a child, we love and praise not that which is, but that which we hope for.

—*Johann Wolfgang von Goethe, poet, and polymath*

The central struggle of parenthood is to let our hopes for our children outweigh our fears.

—***Ellen Goodman, journalist***

By loving them for more than their abilities we show our children that they are much more than the sum of their accomplishments.

—*Eileen Kennedy-Moore, writer and psychologist*

Youth fades, love droops, the leaves of friendship fall,
a mother's secret hope outlives them all.

—*Oliver Wendell Holmes Jr., jurist and poet*

When you have a child, you start to dream of how this kid will grow up and make you proud. The only thing you can predict with 100% certainty is that the reality will diverge somehow from that dream.

—Carol Lynn Pearson, poet and playwright

There is eternal
influence and power
in motherhood.
—Julie B. Beck, religious leader

Parents can only give good advice or put them on the right paths, but the final forming of a person's character lies in their own hands.

—Anne Frank, diarist and Holocaust victim

Children are the only form of immortality that we can be sure of.

—Peter Ustinov, actor and dramatist

If you can remember me, I will be with you always.

—Isabel Allende, novelist

The success of love is in the loving—it is not in the result of loving. Of course it is natural in love to want the best for the other person, but whether it turns out that way or not does not determine the value of what we have done.

—Mother Teresa, nun and Nobel Laureate

Ah! what would the world be to us,
If the children were no more?
We should dread the desert behind us
Worse than the dark before
—Henry Wadsworth Longfellow, poet, from "Children"

I am an onlooker on my daughter's dance, which I made possible because she came through me. . . . I'm not a part of her dance. Yet whenever she takes a pause and needs someone to talk to, I am there. But that special dance with the child and the future is hers.

—Liv Ullmann, actor and director

ACKNOWLEDGMENTS

Much gratitude goes to my editor at Random House Reference, Maren Monitello, who approached me with the idea of preparing a collection of quotes and passages about motherhood. As a new mom, I savored this project. I'm also grateful for the good karma at Jivamukti Café. Sitting there, meditating on a title for this book, I heard a yogi shout the deliciously taboo word "candy!" The room went silent and *Mom Candy* was born.

A universal "thank you" to the hundreds of wise sources from whose novels, poems, guides, blogs, articles, and transcripts I gleaned. Check out these books and articles in the Selected Sources section. Special thanks go to my agent Rick Broadhead for all his support. And this collection wouldn't have been inspired if it were not for my husband, Peter, and my sweet Una Joy.

SELECTED SOURCES

SOURCES LISTED BELOW INCLUDE NOVELS, MEMOIRS, AND INTERVIEWS

BEGINNING

Armstrong: Armstrong, Heather (Dooce). "Bad Mood Baby." *Dooce.com.* http://dooce.com/archives/daily/03_08_2004.html

Bradley: Bradley, Marion Zimmer. *Lady of Avalon*. New York: Penguin, 2007.

Chong: Chong, Tommy. *Cheech & Chong: The Unauthorized Autobiography*. New York: Simon & Schuster, 2009.

Eugenides: Eugenides, Jeffrey. *Middlesex*. New York: Macmillan, 2007.

Foer: Foer, Jonathan Safran. *Eating Animals*. New York: Little, Brown, 2009.

Fonda: Fonda, Jane. *My Life So Far*. New York: Random House, 2005.

Frye: Frye, Soleil Moon. *Happy Chaos*. New York: Penguin, 2011.

Halaby: Halaby, Lisa. *Leap of Faith:Memoirs of an Unexpected Life*. New York: Miramax Books, 2005.

Jay: Jay, Roni. *Zen Meditations on Being Pregnant*. Naperville, Ill.: Sourcebooks, 2000.

Kramer: Kramer, Jacqueline. *Buddha Mom: A Journey Through Mindful Mothering*. New York: Penguin, 2004.

Lamott: Lamott, Anne. *Grace (Eventually): Thoughts on Faith*. New York: Penguin, 2008.

LeShan: LeShan, Eda. *The Conspiracy Against Childhood*. New York: Macmillan, 1971.

Lindbergh: Lindbergh, Anne Morrow. *Gift from the Sea*. New York: Random House, 1975.

Perkins: Perkins, Emily. *Novel About My Wife*. New York: Random House, 2010.

Planck: Planck, Nina. *Real Food for Mother and Baby: The Fertility Diet, Eating for Two, and Baby's First Foods.* New York: Bloomsbury, 2009.

Siddons: Siddons, Anne Rivers. *Colony.* New York: Harper Collins, 1992.

Vietan: Vietan, Cassandra, and Sylvia Boorstein. *Mindful Motherhood: Practical Tools for Staying Sane During Pregnancy and Your Child's First Year.* New York: New Harbinger Publications, 2009.

White: White, E. B., *Charlotte's Web.* New York: HarperCollins, 1951.

Winterson: Winterson, Jeanette. *Sexing the Cherry.* New York: Grove Press, 1989.

Wolf: Wolf, Naomi. *Misconceptions: Truth, Lies, and the Unexpected on the Journey to Motherhood.* New York: Random House, 2003.

Wright: Wright, Jason. *The Wednesday Letters.* Salt Lake City: Shadow Mountain, 2007.

BECOMING

Aaker: Aaker, Linda. *A Woman's Odyssey.* Austin: University of North Texas Press, 1994.

Al Abdullah: MacIntyre, John. *The Amazing Mom Book: Real Facts, Tender Tales, and Thoughts from the Heart.* Naperville, Ill.: Sourcebooks, 2005.

Alba: Goddard, Caroline. "Jessica Alba Talks Mommyhood." http://www.sheknows .com/entertainment/articles/849769/jessica-alba-motherhood-is -overwhelming

Bolding: Lavender, Bee, and Maia Rossini, eds. *Mamaphonic: Balancing Motherhood and Other Creative Acts.* New York: Soft Skull Press, 2004.

Cash: Cash, Rosanne. *Composed: A Memoir.* New York: Penguin, 2010.

Curry: "Interview with Ann Curry." *Working Mother* (February 1994). 14.

De Becker: De Becker, Gavin. *Protecting the Gift: Keeping Children and Teenagers Safe (and Parents Sane).* New York: Random House, 2000.

Dederer: Dederer, Claire. *Poser: My Life in Twenty-three Yoga Poses*. New York: Farrar, Straus & Giroux, 2010.

Dyke: Dyke, Katie van. *Unlikely Truths of Motherhood*. Springville, Utah: Cedar Fort, 2009.

Fey: Fisher, Kelly. "Tina Fey: Working Parents Are 'More Sympathetic.'" *Pop Eater*, March 10, 2011. http://www.popeater.com/2011/03/10/tina-fey-working-parents-sympathetic

Fonda: Fonda, Jane. *My Life So Far*. New York: Random House, 2005.

Groff: Groff, Lauren. *Delicate Edible Birds and Other Stories*. New York: Hyperion, 2009.

Gyllenhaal: Pilmer, Martyn. "'I Have a Bit of the Hippie Mum in Me': Maggie Gyllenhaal on Juggling Acting with Motherhood." *The Daily Mail*, September 14, 2009. http://www.dailymail.co.uk/home/you/article-1211959/Maggie-Gyllenhaal-juggling-acting-motherhood-I-bit-hippie-mum-me.html

Merzenich: Ellison, Katherine. *The Mommy Brain: How Motherhood Makes Us Smarter*. New York: Basic Books, 2005.

Moore: Moore, Beth, and Dale McCleskey. *Jesus, the One and Only*. Nashville, Tenn.: B&H Publishing, 2002.

O'Mara: Flower, Hilary. Foreword by Peggy O'Mara. *Adventures in Tandem Nursing: Breastfeeding During Pregnancy and Beyond*. New York: La Leche League, 2003.

Picoult: Picoult, Jodi. *Vanishing Acts*. New York: Simon & Schuster, 2005.

Richesin: Richesin, Andrea. *Because I Love Her: 34 Women Writers Reflect on the Mother-Daughter Bond*. New York: Harlequin, 2009.

Sarah: Stonehouse, Cathy, ed. *Double Lives: Writing and Motherhood*. Toronto: McGill-Queen's Press, 2008.

Shields: Shields, Brooke. *Down Came the Rain*. New York: Hyperion, 2005.

Wilkinson: Wilkinson, Kendra. *Sliding into Home*. New York: Simon & Schuster, 2010.

BOND

Ackerman: Ackerman, Diane. "The Brain on Love." The New York Times, March 24, 2012. http://opinionator.blogs.nytimes.com/2012/03/24/the-brain-on-love

Ackerman: Ackerman, Diane. *A Natural History of Love.* New York: Random House, 1994.

Ainsworth: Ainsworth, Jerry. *Love & Health: Twelve Physical, Mental and Spiritual Ingredients of Health.* Victoria, B.C.: Trafford, 2006.

Blum: Blum, Deborah. *Love at Goon Park.* New York: Basic Books, 2002.

Curry: Carter, Gayle. "Ann Curry's Best Tips for Working Moms." *USA Weekend,* June 26, 2011. http://www.usaweekend.com/article/20110701/ENTERTAINMENT 05/307010007/Ann-Curry-s-best-tips-working-moms

Goldberg: Goldberg, Carey, B. Jones, and P. Ferdinand. *Three Wishes: A True Story of Good Friends, Crushing Heartbreak, and Astonishing Luck on Our Way to Love and Motherhood.* New York: Little, Brown, 2010.

Hill: Hill, Milli. "Love Is the Answer: Ten Creative Ways to Strengthen Attachment." *Mamamule,* March 3, 2012. http://mamamule.blogspot.com/2012/02/love-is -answer-ten-creative-ways-to.html

Kaplan: Kaplan, Louise. *Oneness and Separateness: From Infant to Individual.* New York: Simon & Schuster, 1978.

Karr-Morse: Karr-Morse, Robin, with Meredith Riley. *Scared Sick: The Role of Childhood Trauma in Adult Disease.* New York: Basic Books, 2012.

Kasi: Kasi, Charlotte. *Women, Sex, and Addiction: A Search for Love and Power.* New York: HarperCollins, 1990.

McKay: Dyke, Katie van. *Unlikely Truths of Motherhood.* Springville, Utah: Cedar Fort, 2009.

Picoult: Picoult, Jodi. *Handle With Care.* New York: Simon & Schuster, 2009.

Picoult: Picoult, Jodi. *Vanishing Acts.* New York: Simon & Schuster, 2005.

Rich: Rich, Adrienne. *Of Woman Born*. New York: Norton, 1995.

Rilke: Rilke, Rainer Maria. *Letters*. New York: W. W. Norton, 1945.

DELICIOUS

Barry: Barry, Dave. *Babies & Other Hazards of Sex*. New York: St. Martin's, 1984.

Berger: Berger, Elizabeth. *Raising Kids with Character: Developing Trust and Personal Integrity in Children*. Oxford: Rowman & Littlefield, 1999.

Center: Center, Katherine. *The Bright Side of Disaster*. New York: Random House, 2007.

Coolidge: Coolidge, Susan. *What Katy Did Next*. London: Objective Systems, 2006.

Crittenden: Crittenden, Danielle. *What Our Mothers Didn't Tell Us: Why Happiness Eludes the Modern Woman*. New York: Simon & Schuster, 1999.

Day: Day, Christina. "Baby Love," *Working Mother* (November 1986). 190.

Edwards: Edwards, Jaroldeen. *Things I Wish I'd Known Sooner: Personal Discoveries of a Mother of Twelve*. New York: Pocket Books, 1998.

Gabaldon: Gabaldon, Diana. *Dragonfly in Amber*. New York: Random House, 1992.

Gordon: Gordon, Mary. *Men and Angels*. New York: Random House, 1986.

Gregory: Gregory, Philippa. *Wideacre*. New York: Simon & Schuster, 1987.

Himnefield: Himnefield, Joyce. *In Hovering Flight*. Denver: Unbridled Books, 2008.

Ivey: Ivey, Eowyn. *The Snow Child*. New York: Little, Brown, 2012.

Karr: Karr, Mary. *Lit: A Memoir*. New York: HarperCollins, 2009.

Keller: Peri, Camille, and Kate Moses. *Mothers Who Think: Tales of Real-life Parenthood*. New York: Random House, 1999.

Kingsolver: Kingsolver, Barbara. *The Poisonwood Bible*. New York: HarperCollins, 1999.

Lafser: Lafser, Christine. *Longing for My Child: Reflections for Parents and Siblings After a Child's Death*. Chicago: Loyola Press, 2002.

Picoult: Picoult, Jodi. *Perfect Match*. New York: Simon & Schuster, 2002.

Schwarzer: Schwarzer, Elizabeth Soutter. *Motherhood Is Not for Wimps: No Answers, Just Stories*. New York: AuthorHouse, 2006.

Stefani: Gordon, Jane. "Gwen Stefani Struggles With Motherhood and Career." *Daily Mail Online*. September 7, 2001.

ONE & ONLY

Albom: Albom, Mitch. *For One More Day*. New York: HarperCollins, 2006.

Cleese: Cleese, Alyce Faye. *How to Manage Your Mother: Understanding the Most Difficult, Complicated and Fascinating Relationship in Your Life*. New York: HarperCollins, 2000.

Gibran: Gibran, Kahlil. *Wings of Thought*. New York: Open Road Integrated Media, 1973.

Hathaway: Hathaway, Katherine Butler. *The Little Locksmith: A Memoir*. 1943; repr. New York: The Feminist Press, 2000.

Jemisin: Jemisin, N. K. *The Hundred Thousand Kingdoms*. New York: Hachette, 2010.

Jong: Jong, Erica. *Fear of Fifty: A Midlife Memoir*. New York: Penguin, 1994.

Krauss: Krauss, Nicole. *The History of Love*. New York: W. W. Norton, 2005.

Trigiani: Trigiani, Adriana. *Big Stone Gap*. New York: Ballantine, 2000.

Trigiani: Trigiani, Adriana. *Don't Sing at the Table: Life Lessons from My Grandmothers*. New York: HarperCollins, 2010.

DELIGHT

Berk: Berk, Brett. *The Gay Uncle's Guide to Parenting*. New York: Three Rivers Press, 2008.

Buzbee: Buzbee, Lewis. *The Yellow-Lighted Bookshop: A Memoir, A History*. Saint Paul, Minn.: Graywolf, 2006.

Callahan: Callahan, Alice. "My Child is a Scientist." *Science of Mom*. Feb 16, 2012. http://scienceofmom.com/tag/toddler-in-nature/

Dimof: Steinberg, Eden, ed. *Finding Your Inner Mama*. New York: Random House, 2003; Boston: Shambhala, 2005.

Emerson: Emerson Ralph Waldo. *The complete works of Ralph Waldo Emerson*. New York: Houghton Mifflin, 1904.

Hendrickson: Hendrickson, Kirstin. *Squint Mom*. March 1, 2012. http://www.squintmom.com/thoughts-and-commentary/things-i-ponder/phthursday-philosophy-auguries-of-innocence

LeCarre: LeCarre, John. *Our Game*. New York: Knopf, 1995.

Mason: Mason, Mike. *The Mystery of Children*. Colorado Springs: Waterbrook Press, 2001.

Quindlen: Quindlen, Anna. "Public & Private; Enough Bookshelves." *The New York Times*. August 7, 1991. http://www.nytimes.com/1991/08/07/opinion/public-private-enough-bookshelves.html

Quindlen: Quindlen, Anna. *Thinking Out Loud: On the Personal, the Political, the Public and the Private*. New York: Random House, 2003.

Robbins: Robbins, Tom. *Still Life with Woodpecker*. New York: Bantam Books, 1980.

HEART

Coben: Coben, Harlan. *Caught*. New York: Penguin, 2010.

Osho: Osho. *Compassion: The Ultimate Flowering of Love*. New York: Macmillan, 2007.

Picoult: Picoult, Jodi. *Perfect Match*. New York: Washington Square Press, 2003.

Shusterman: Shusterman, Neal. *Unwind*. New York: Simon & Schuster, 2007.

Baker: Baker, Tiffany. *The Little Giant of Aberdeen County*. New York: Hachette, 2009.

Souljah: Souljah, Sister. *Midnight and the Meaning of Love*. New York: Simon & Schuster, 2011.

INFLUENCE

Casals: Edelman, Marian. *I Can Make a Difference: A Treasury to Inspire Our Children.* New York: HarperCollins, 2005.

Foer: Foer, Jonathan Safran. *Extremely Loud and Incredibly Close.* New York: Houghton Mifflin, 2005.

Ginzburg: Ginzburg, Natalia. *The Little Virtues.* New York: Arcade Publishing, 1989.

Johnson: Johnson, Nicole. *The Invisible Woman: A Special Story for Mothers.* New York: Thomas Nelson, 2005.

Lamott: Lamott, Anne. *Bird by Bird: Some Instructions on Writing and Life.* New York: Random House, 1994.

Moore: Relter, Amy. "Motherhood Doesn't Wipe Out the Person That You Are." *Babble,* April 2, 2011. http://www.babble.com/Celebrity/celebrity-moms/Julianne -Moore-talks-about-Freckleface-Strawberry-and-her-kids

Sarandon: Sarandon, Susan. "Speaking Her Mind." *The Reader's Digest* (August 2002): 79.

Sturges: Sturges, Tom. "The Parking Lot Rules." *Best Life* (June 2008): 130.

Winterson: Winterson, Jeanette. *The Stone Gods.* New York: Random House, 2007.

TIME

Ashworth: Ashworth, Trisha, and Amy Nobile. *I Was a Really Good Mom Before I Had Kids: Reinventing Modern Motherhood.* San Francisco: Chronicle Books, 2007.

Berg: Berg, Elizabeth. *The Art of Mending.* New York: Random House, 2004.

Evans: Evans, Richard Paul. *The Christmas Box Miracle: My Spiritual Journey of Destiny, Healing and Hope.* New York: Simon & Schuster, 2001.

Fowler: Hershey, Jennifer, ed. *Full Spectrum 5.* New York: Spectra, 2005.

Gabaldon: Galbaldon, Diana. *Voyager.* New York: Delta, 2001.

Gilbert: Senior, Jennifer. "All Joy and No Fun." New York, July 4, 2010. http://nymag.com/news/features/67024

Hill: Hill, Milli. "While I Nurse You To Sleep." *Mamamule*, March 9, 2012. http://mamamule.blogspot.com/2012/03/while-i-nurse-you-to-sleep.html

Kenison: Kenison, Katrina. *The Gift of an Ordinary Day: A Mother's Memoir*. New York: Hachette, 2009.

Moran: Moran, Victoria. *Younger by the Day: 365 Ways to Rejuvenate Your Body and Revitalize Your Spirit*. New York: Harper One, 2004.

Napthali: Napthali, Sarah. *Buddhism for Mothers: A Calm Approach to Caring for Yourself and Your Child*. Crows Nest, Australia: Allen & Unwin, 2003.

Rubin: Francis, Meagan. "The Days Are Long, the Years Are Short: Happy Mom Interview with Gretchen Rubin of The Happiness Project." September 20, 2010. http://thehappiestmom.com/2010/09/the-days-are-long-the-years-are-short-qa-with-gretchen-rubin-of-the-happiness-project/

Tropper: Tropper. Jonathan. *This Is Where I Leave You*. New York: Penguin, 2009.

Twain: Twain, Mark. *A Connecticut Yankee in King Arthur's Court*. New York: Greenwich House, 1890.

Warren: Warren, Rick. *The Purpose Driven Life: What on Earth Am I Here For?* Grand Rapids, Mich.: Zondervan, 2002.

Woolf: Woolf, Virginia. *To the Lighthouse*. 1927; repr. New York: Houghton Mifflin, 1955.

Zabat-Kinn: Zabat-Kinn, Jon. *Wherever You Go, There You Are: Mindfulness Meditation in Everyday Life*. New York: Hyperion, 1994.

BALANCE

Ball: Ball, Donna. *At Home on Ladybug Farm*. New York: Penguin, 2009.

Burke: Burke, Brooke. *The Naked Mom*. New York: Penguin, 2012.

Creech: Creech, Sharon. *Walk Two Moons*. New York: HarperCollins, 1994.

DeVivo: Gresik, Alison. "Hours for Art Interview with Miki DeVivo." December 15, 2011. http://www.gresik.ca/2011/12/hours-for-art-interview-with-miki-devivo/

DiFranco: Nathman, Avital. "Mom & Pop Culture: An Interview with Ani DiFranco." *Bitch*, December 22, 2011. http://bitchmagazine.org/post/mom-pop-culture-an-interview-with-ani-difranco

Druckerman: Cohen, Shawna. "Pamela Druckerman Tells Mommyish Why French Parents Do It Right." *Mommyish*, February 11, 2011. http://mommyish.com/childrearing/pamela-druckerman-bringing-up-bebe-950/

Gimenez Smith: Gimenez Smith, Carmen. *Bring Down the Little Birds: On Mothering, Art, Work, and Everything Else.* Phoenix: University of Arizona Press, 2010.

Lucci: Lucci, Susan. *All My Life.* New York: HarperCollins, 2011.

Picoult: Picoult, Jodi. *My Sister's Keeper.* New York: Simon & Schuster, 2004.

Prose: Prose, Francine. "I Heard My Son Say 'Mom Hardly Does Anything.'" *Working Mother* (January 1988): 54.

Rowling: Weir, Margaret. "Of Magic and Single Motherhood," Salon.com. Mar 13, 1999. http://www.salon.com/writer/margaret_weir/

Thurman: "Uma Thurman Tackles New Role." Rolemommy.com. Oct 23, 2009. http://www.rolemommy.com/blog/uma-thurman-tackles-new-role-m.php

Waldman: Waldman, Ayelet. *Bad Mother: A Chronicle of Maternal Crimes, Minor Calamities.* New York: Random House, 2009.

LAUGH

Seinfeld: Holland, Lila. "Jerry Seinfeld and Wife Welcome Third Child." http://www.tv.com/news/jerry-seinfeld-and-wife-welcome-third-child-574

GIFTS

Adams: "Yolanda Adams." http://www.laphil.com/philpedia/artist-detail.cfm?id=1366

Coelho: Coelho, Paulo. *The Pilgrimage*. New York: HarperCollins, 1986.

Dayton: *Daily Affirmations for Parents*. New York: Innerlook, 1992.

Ellison: Ellison, Katherine. "The Mind of the Harried Mom." *Working Mother* (February 2003): 48

Fadiman: Fadiman, Anne. *At Large and At Small: Familiar Essays*. New York: Macmillan, 2007.

Fuchs-Kreimer: Fuchs-Kreimer, Nancy. *Parenting as a Spiritual Journey*. Woodstock, N.Y.: Jewish Lights Publishing, 1998.

Hanh: Hanh. Thich Nhat. *Being Peace*. Sydney: ReadHowYouWant, 2008.

Jong: Jong, Erica. *Fear of Fifty: A Midlife Memoir*. New York: Penguin, 1994.

Kabat-Zinn: Kabat-Zinn, Jon. *Wherever You Go, There You Are: Mindfulness Meditation in Everyday Life*. New York: Hyperion, 1994.

Lambert: Ellison, Katherine. "The Mind of the Harried Mom." *Working Mother* (February 2003): 48.

Lima: Castillo, Amaris. "EXCLUSIVE: Alessandra Ambrosio & Adriana Lima on Modeling & Motherhood." *Latina*, November 11, 2011. http://www.latina.com/lifestyle/parenting/exclusive-alessandra-ambrosio-adriana-lima-modeling-motherhood

Madonna: Born, Matt. "I Was So Selfish, Motherhood Has Mellowed Me." *The Telegraph*, September 4, 2002. http://www.telegraph.co.uk/news/uknews/1406194/I-was-so-selfish-motherhood-has-mellowed-me.html

Martin: Chefas, Stephanie. "An Interview with Lily Mae Martin." *Hi-Fructose*. http://hifructose.com/index.php/the-blog/2110-an-interview-with-lily-mae-martin

Messing: Carillo, Jenny Cooney. *InStyle*, March 2005. http://www.jennycooney.com/messing.html

Moses: Iverson, Rachel. "An Interview with Kate Moses." *Literary Mama*, March 9, 2004. http://www.literarymama.com/profiles/archives/2004/03/kate-moses.html

Pelosi: Hoyt, Carolyn. "A Friend in the House." *Working Mother* (May 2002): 22.

Perez: Perez, Cristina. *Living by Los Dichos: Advice from a Mother to a Daughter.* New York: Simon & Schuster, 2006.

Phillips: Scotch, Allison Winn. 15 Sept 2011. "Six Questions With Busy Philipps." Parents, September 15, 2011. http://www.parents.com/blogs/balance-sheet/2011/09/15/celebrity/six-questions-with-busy-philipps-2

Taitz: Taitz, Sonia. *Mothering Heights.* New York: Berkley, 1994.

Wingate: Wingate, Lisa. *Tending Roses.* New York: Penguin, 2001.

Winokur: "Celebs on Motherhood." *Redbook.* http://www.redbookmag.com/fun-contests/celebrity/celebrity-moms#slide-3

NURTURE

Angelidis: Angelidis, Ellenore. "Complete Trust—Motherhood Reward and Responsibility." http://balancingmotherhoodcareer.blogspot.com/2011/09/complete-trust-motherhood-reward-and.html

Bee: Couch, Christina. "Samantha Bee: An Exclusive Interview with the *Daily Show* Star and Mother of Two." *Babble.* http://babble.com/Celebrity/celebrity-style/samantha-bee-the-daily-show-and-her-kids

Brizendine: Brizendine, Louann. *The Female Brain.* New York: Random House, 2006.

Brown: Brown, Brené. *The Gifts of Imperfection.* Center City, Minn.: Hazelden, 2010.

Coleman: Coleman, Rowan. "Interview with Rowan Coleman." Authors: Simon & Schuster. http://authors.simonandschuster.com/Rowan-Coleman/39849884/interview/1

Harper: Harper, Frances. "The Two Offers." *The Anglo-African Magazine.* Sept-Oct 1859.

Hinckley: Hinckley, Marjorie. *Small and Simple Things.* Salt Lake City: Deseret, 2003.

Hunt: Hunt, Gladys. *Honey for a Child's Heart: The Imaginative Use of Books in Family Life.* Grand Rapids, Mich.: Zondervan, 2010.

Keillor: Keillor, Garrison. "The Mysteries of Prom Night." *A Prairie Home Companion,* May 15, 2000.

Kent: Kent, Kathleen. *The Heretic's Daughter.* New York: Little, Brown, 2008.

McClure: McClure, Vimala. "The Tao of Motherhood: An Interview with Vimala McClure." *New World Library,* May 5, 2011. http://newworldlibrary.com/NewWorld LibraryUnshelved/tabid/767/articleType/ArticleView/articleId/69/The-Tao -of-Motherhood-An-Interview-with-Vimala-McClure.aspx

Peck: Peck, Scott. *The Road Less Traveled.* New York: HarperCollins, 2003.

Ridley: Ridley, Matt. *The Red Queen: Sex and the Evolution of Human Nature.* New York: HarperCollins, 2003. http://prairiehome.publicradio.org/features/ deskofgk/000515__time.shtml

Sage: Sage, Sandra. *Love on a Plate.* Bloomington, Ind.: AuthorHouse, 2007.

STRENGTH

Albom: Albom, Mitch. *For One More Day.* New York: Hyperion, 2006.

Barrie: Barrie, James. *Peter Pan.* New York: Broadway Books, 2011.

Blanchett: Estall, Lisa. "Cate Blanchett & Family: Sightseeing In Paris." *Celebrity Baby Scoop,* April 3, 2012. http://celebritybabyscoop.com/2012/04/03/cate -blanchett

Corrigan: Corrigan, Kelly. *Lift.* New York: Hyperion, 2010.

Elliot: Elliot, Sarah. *These Is My Words: The Diary of Sarah Agnes Prine, 1881–1901.* New York: HarperCollins, 1998.

Huffington: Huffington, Arianna. "Fearless and Fabulous." *Washington Post,* December 5, 2006. http://www.washingtonpost.com/wp-dyn/content/ article/2006/12/05/AR2006120500907.html

Hunt: Hunt, Helen. "I've Stopped Trying to Get Everything Right: Interview with Helen Hunt About Her New Movie and Her Family." *Redbook.* http://www.redbookmag .com/fun-contests/celebrity/helen-hunt-interview 3#ixzz1rrcBXR87

Kelly: Kelly, Marguerite, and Parsons, Elia. *Mother's Almanac*. New York: Main Street Books, 1975.

Kenison: Kenison, Katrina. *The Gift of an Ordinary Day: A Mother's Memoir*. New York: Hachette, 2009.

Mead-Ferro: Mead-Ferro, Muffy. *Confessions of a Slacker Mom*. New York: Perseus, 2004.

Pasha: Kamran, Pasha. *Mother of the Believers: A Novel of the Birth of Islam*. New York: Simon & Schuster, 2009.

Schlesinger: Schlesinger, Laura. *In Praise of Stay-At-Home Moms*. New York: Harper-Collins, 2009.

Simon: Simon, Scott. *Baby, We Were Meant for Each Other: In Praise of Adoption*. New York: Random House, 2010.

White: White, E. B., *Charlotte's Web*. New York: HarperCollins, 1951.

Zettel: Zettel, Sarah. *Dust Girl*. New York: Random House, 2012.

PERFECTION

Alba: Margaret, Mary. "Work Takes a Backseat to Motherhood." *Parade*, January 20, 2012. http://www.parade.com/celebrity/celebrity-parade/2012/01/20-jessica-alba.html

Amanpour: Amanpour, Christiane. "To Thine Own Self Be True—and Other Eternal Truths." *Huffington Post*, October 3, 2011. http://www.huffingtonpost.com/christiane-amanpour/to-thine-own-self-be-true__b__990985.html

Dessen: Dessen, Sarah. *This Lullaby*. New York: Penguin, 2002.

Hawn: Hawn, Goldie. 10 Mindful Minutes. New York: Penguin, 2011.

Iyengar: Iyengar, Sheena. *The Art of Choosing*. New York: Hachette, 2011.

Kenyon: Kenyon, Sherrilyn. *Devil May Cry: A Dark-Hunter Novel*. New York: Macmillan, 2008.

Lawrence: Howard, Cori, ed. *Between Interruptions: 28 Women Tell the Truth About Motherhood.* Bloomington, Ind.: iUniverse, 2011.

Millman: Millman, Dan. *Body Mind Mastery: Creating Success in Sport and Life.* Novato, Calif.: New World Library, 1999.

Moran: Moran, Victoria. *Younger by the Day: 365 Ways to Rejuvenate Your Body and Revitalize Your Spirit.* New York: HarperCollins, 2004.

Nordeman: Elliot, Belinda. "Nichole Nordeman on Marriage and Motherhood." http://www.cbn.com/cbnmusic/interviews/elliott_nicholenordeman042006.aspx

Pausch: Pausch, Randy. *The Last Lecture.* New York: Hyperion, 2008.

Picoult: Picoult, Jodi. *House Rules.* New York: Simon & Schuster, 2010.

Pillay: Pillay, Srini. "What a Psychiatrist Learned During Therapy Sessions with Mothers." http://www.kevinmd.com/blog/2011/08/psychiatrist-learned-therapy-sessions-mothers.html

Rubin: Rubin, Gretchen. *The Happiness Project.* New York: HarperCollins, 2009.

Sandberg: Weinreb, Ellen. "Sheryl Sandberg and Motherhood: Why Kids Help Us Become Better Executives." *Forbes*, September 30, 2001. http://www.forbes.com/sites/work-in-progress/2011/09/30/sheryl-sandberg-and-motherhood-why-kids-help-us-become-better-executives

Waldman: Waldman, Ayelet. *Bad Mother: A Chronicle of Maternal Crimes, Minor Calamities.* New York: Random House, 2009.

Watson: Balint, Molly. "War Horse's Emily Watson on Motherhood." *BabyCenter*, December 23, 2011. http://blogs.babycenter.com/celebrities/war-horses-emily-watson-on-motherhood

Woodman: Woodman, Sue. "Seven Habits of Smart Moms," *McCalls*, May 13, 1995.

Xue: Xue Xinran. *The Good Women of China: Hidden Voices.* New York: Random House, 2003.

LIFESAVERS

Baadsgaard: Baadsgaard, Janene Wolsey. *For Every Mother*. Salt Lake City: Deseret, 2011.

Berg: Berg, Elizabeth. *The Pull of the Moon*. New York: Random House, 1996.

Bergren: Bergren, Lisa. *Life on Planet Mom: A Down-to-Earth Guide to Your Changing Relationships*. Grand Rapids, Mich.: Revell, 2009.

Bialik: Bialik, Mayim. *Beyond the Sling: A Real-Life Guide to Raising Confident, Loving Children*. New York: Simon & Schuster, 2012.

Bloom: Nathan, Bradi. "Interview with Lisa Bloom; Attorney and Award-Winning journalist." *My Work Butterfly*, August 31, 2009. http://www.myworkbutterfly.com/profiles/blogs/interview-with-lisa-bloom

Butcher: Butcher, Jim. *Proven Guilty*. New York: Penguin, 2007.

Casarjian: Casarjian, Bethany, and Diane Dillon. *Mommy Mantras: Affirmations and Insights to Keep You From Losing Your Mind*. New York: Random House, 2006.

Craik: Craik, Dinah. *A Life for a Life*. New York: B. Taucnitz, 1859.

Erdrich: Erdrich, Louise. *The Blue Jay's Dance: A Memoir of Early Motherhood*. New York: HarperCollins, 2010.

Foer: Foer, Jonathan Safran. *Everything Is Illuminated*. New York: Houghton Mifflin, 2002.

Garner: Robertson, Carolyn. "Jennifer Garner: I Think That My Kids' Lives Are Pretty Normal." *Celebrity Baby Scoop*, September 28, 2009. http://www.celebritybabyscoop.com/2009/09/28/jennifer-garner-i-think-that-my-kids-lives-are-pretty-normal

Hannah: Hannah, Kristen. *Firefly Lane*. New York: Macmillan, 2009.

Hayek: Reed, Sheri. "Salma Hayek Is the Coolest Mom on the Planet (Exclusive Interview)." *Cafe Mom*, October 28, 2011. http://thestir.cafemom.com/baby/125827/salma_hayek_is_the_coolest

Heigl: "It's a Family Affair." *The Daily Mail*, October 13, 2010. http://www.dailymail.co.uk/tvshowbiz/article-1320224/Katherine-Heigl-Josh-Kelley-enjoy-day-adorable-daughter-Naleigh.html

Jong: Jong, Erica. "Mother Madness." *The Wall Street Journal*, November 6, 2010. http://online.wsj.com/article/SB10001424052748704462704575590603553674296.html

Kaplan: Kaplan, Louise. *Oneness and Separateness: From Infant to Individual*. New York: Simon & Schuster, 1998.

Kinsey: Kinsey, Angela. "Interview with Angela Kinsey," *What to Expect*, January 7, 2011. http://www.whattoexpect.com/blogs/skincareandbeauty/interview-with-angela-kinsey

Klum: Smith, Sassy. "Heidi Klum Talks Family & Baby Number Four," Babble, April 27, 2009. http://www.babble.com/CS/blogs/famecrawler/archive/2009/04/27/heidi-klum-talks-family-amp-baby-number-four.aspx

Lennon: Wenner, Jann. *Lennon Remembers*. New York: Verso, 1971.

Meyerhoff: Ginsberg, Susan, ed. *Family Wisdom*. New York: Columbia University Press. 1996.

Osteen: Osteen, Joel. *Your Best Life Now: 7 Steps to Living at Your Full Potential*. New York: Simon & Schuster, 2004.

Quindlen: Quindlen, Anna. *Loud and Clear*. New York: Random House, 2004.

Smith: Smith, Jada Pinkett. "Jada Pinkett Smith." *Working Mother*, October 2008. http://www.workingmother.com/2008/10/home/jada-pinkett-smith

Steingraber: Steingraber, Sandra. *Having Faith*. New York: Da Capo, 2001.

Vonnegut: Vonnegut, Kurt. *God Bless You, Dr. Kevorkian*. New York: Simon & Schuster, 2001.

RENEWAL

Amos: A.D., Catherine. "Artist 'n' Artist: Catherine AD meets Tori Amos." *Drownedin Sound.com*, May 29, 2009. http://drownedinsound.com/in_depth/4136866

Castillo: Castillo, Brooke. *If I'm So Smart, Why Can't I Lose Weight?* Seattle: Book-Surge, 2006.

Crawford: Bell, Carrie. "Celebrity Mom Interview Cindy Crawford. *Parents.com*, March 2006. http://www.parents.com/parenting/celebrity-parents/celebrity-mom-interview-cindy-crawford/

Friday: Friday, Nancy. *My Mother/My Self*. New York: Delta, 1977.

Gould: Gould, Roger. *Transformations*. New York: Simon & Schuster, 1978.

Ireland: Perry, Katie. "A Beautiful Life." *Carmel*, Holiday 2009. http://www.carmel magazine.com/archive/09ho/kathy-ireland.shtml

Lessing: Lessing, Doris. *A Man and Two Women*. New York: Simon & Schuster, 1984.

Moore: Moore, Thomas. *The Re-Enchantment of Everyday Life*. New York: HarperCollins, 1996.

Peet: "Amanda Peet on Motherhood." *People*, November 18, 2009. http://celebrityba bies.people.com/2009/11/18/amanda-peet-on-motherhood-put-on-your-own-oxygen-mask-first/

Quest: Quest, Penelope. *Reiki for Life*. New York: Penguin, 2010.

Sarah: Stonehouse, Cathy, ed. *Double Lives: Writing and Motherhood*. Toronto: McGill-Queen's Press, 2008.

RELEASE

Albom: Albom, Mitch. *The Five People You Meet in Heaven*. New York: Hyperion, 2003.

Armstrong: Armstrong, Heather. "You can't always get what you want." *Dooce.com*. Nov 15, 2005. http://dooce.com/archives/daily/11_15_2005.html

Barrie: Barrie, James. *Peter Pan*. Middlesex, U.K.: Echo Library, 1911.

Fey: "Tina Fey Reveals All (And Then Some) In 'Bossypants.'" http://www.npr.org/2011/04/13/135247195/tina-fey-reveals-all-and-then-some-in-bossypants

Gopnik: Gopnik, Allison. *The Philosophical Baby*. New York: Macmillan, 2009.

Kingsolver: Kingsolver, Barbara. *Animal Dreams*. New York: HarperCollins, 1991.

Kingsolver: Kingsolver, Barbara. *Pigs in Heaven*. New York: HarperCollins, 1994.

Krauss: Krauss, Nicole. *The History of Love*. New York: W. W. Norton, 2011.

Morrison: Morrison, Toni. *Beloved*. New York: Knopf, 1987.

Richesin: Richesin, Andrea. *Because I Love Her: 34 Women Writers Reflect on the Mother-Daughter Bond*. New York: Harlequin, 2009.

See: See, Lisa. *Dreams of Joy*. New York: Random House, 2011.

Wheeler: Wheeler, Maureen. *Unlikely Destinations*. Hong Kong: Periplus, 2007.

LEGACY

Allende: Allende, Isabel. *Eva Luna*. New York: Knopf, 1989.

Atwood: Atwood, Margaret. *The Penelopiad: The Myth of Penelope and Odysseus*. New York: Canongate, 2005.

Cavoukian: Cavoukian, Raffi. "A Covenant for Honoring Children." http://www.raffinews.com/child-honouring/covenant-principles

Coward: Payn, Graham, ed. *The Noël Coward Diaries*. New York: Da Capo, 1982.

Fey: Fey, Tina. *Bossypants*. New York: Hachette, 2011.

Ginsberg: Ginsberg, Debra. *Raising Blaze: Bringing Up an Extraordinary Son in an Ordinary World*. New York: HarperCollins, 2002.

Graffin: Graffin, Greg. *Anarchy Evolution: Faith, Science, and Bad Religion in a World Without God*. New York: HarperCollins, 2010.

Griffioen: Armstrong, Heather. *Things I Learned About My Dad (in Therapy): Essays*. New York: Kensington, 2008.

Hale: Hale, Shannon. *Book of a Thousand Days*. New York: Bloomsbury, 2007.

Hayek: Martin, Crystal. "Salma Hayek's Aha! Moment: Discovering My True Motivation." *O Magazine*, December 2011. http://www.oprah.com/spirit/Salma-Hayek -Interview-Salma-Hayek-on-Shrek-Spin-Off

Jong: Jong, Erica. *How to Save Your Own Life*. New York: Penguin, 1977.

Kingsolver: Kingsolver, Barbara. *Animal, Vegetable, Miracle: A Year of Food Life*. New York: HarperCollins, 2007.

Kingsolver: Kingsolver, Barbara. *The Bean Trees*. New York: HarperCollins, 1988.

Pausch: Pausch: Pausch, Randy. *The Last Lecture*. New York: Hyperion, 2008.

Pearson: Pearson, Carol Lynn. *Goodbye, I Love You*. Springville, Utah: Cedar Fort, 2006.

Picoult: Picoult, Jodi. *Handle with Care*. New York: Simon & Schuster, 2009.

Quindlen: Quindlen, Anna. *Thinking Out Loud: On the Personal, the Political, the Public and the Private*. New York: Random House, 2003.

Sanchez: Sanchez, Sonia. *Shake Loose My Skin: New and Selected Poems*. Boston: Beacon Press, 1999.

Sittenfeld: Sittenfeld, Curtis. *American Wife*. New York: Random House, 2008.

Turner: Turner, Nancy. *These Is My Words: The Diary of Sarah Agnes Prine, 1881– 1901*. New York: HarperCollins, 1998.

SPEAKER LIST

BEGINNINGS

Mary Mason
Don Herold
Barbara Christine Seifert
Roni Jay
Maureen Hawkins
Elizabeth Stone
E.B. White
Jane Fonda
Robert Anton Wilson
Natalie Portman
Jeffrey Eugenides
Naomi Wolf
Jacqueline Kramer
Emily Perkins
William Sears
Cassandra Vietan and
   Sylvia Boorstein
Brett Kiellerop
Harriette Hartigan
Nina Planck
Jeanette Winterson
Marion Zimmer Bradley
Anne Rivers Siddons
Anne Morrow Lindbergh

Judy Ford
Madeleine L'Engle
Percy Bysshe Shelley
Pablo Casals
Gisele Bündchen
Vincent van Gogh
Heather Armstrong
   (Dooce)
Elizabeth C. Bunce
Johnny Depp
George MacDonald
Anne Lamott
Lisa Hajeeb Halaby (Queen
   Noor)
Tommy Chong
Eda J. LeShan
Soleil Moon Frye
Jason F. Wright
George Bernard Shaw
American proverb
Jonathan Safran Foer
William MacNeile Dixon

BECOMING

Maya Angelou
Erma Bombeck

Osho
Marni Jackson
George Eliot
Lisa Gardner
Kim Gaines Eckert
Cheryl Lacey Donovan
Muffy Bolding
Katie van Dyke
Julie Walters
Hillary Rodham Clinton
Jane Fonda
Suzanne Somers
Terri Guillemets
Rosanne Cash
Debra Gilbert Rosenberg
Charles Du Bos
Céline Dion
Jodi Picoult
Claire Dederer
Lama Tsultrim Allione
Roseanne Barr
Linda Poindexter
Brooke Shields
David Sheff
Anne Lamott

Jessica Lange
Beth Moore and Dale McCleskey
Mary Howitt
Jodi Picoult
Andrea Richesin
Sophia Loren
Kate Winslet
Jessica Alba
Kendra Wilkinson
Maggie Gyllenhaal
Michael Merzenich
Lauren Groff
Peggy O'Mara
Korean proverb
Kate Winslet
Holly Marie Combs
Erma Bombeck
Gavin de Becker
Ann Curry
Tina Fey
Rania Al Abdullah
Charlotte Gray
Robyn Sarah
Halle Berry
Erica Jong
Linda Aaker

BOND

Fran Lebowitz

Milli Hill
Jodi Picoult
Benjamin Spock
Jessica Zucker
Shirley MacLaine
Marilynne Robinson
Adrienne Rich
Erica Eisdorfer
Kathryn Stockett
Diane Ackerman
Jeff Foxworthy
Deborah Blum
Gail Tsukiyama
Margaret Culkin Banning
Marjorie Holmes
Jodi Picoult
Diane Ackerman
Ward Schumaker
Gabriel García Márquez
David O. McKay
C.S. Lewis
Karen Maezen Miller
Erica Jong
Lucy Maud Montgomery
Washington Irving
Vicki Lansky
Louise J. Kaplan
Jerry Ainsworth
Robin Karr-Morse
William D. Tammeus

Ann Curry
Tori Spelling
Carey Goldberg
Eartha Kitt
Strickland Gillilan
Paolo Ruffini
Theodor Reik
Charlotte Gray
George Eliot
Edmund Clarence Stedman
Rainer Maria Rilke
Max Lucado
Charlotte Kasi

DELICIOUS

Leo Gallagher
Danielle Crittenden
Christina Day
Mary Gordon
Elizabeth Berger
Algernon Charles Swinburne
John Banville
Philippa Gregory
Eowyn Ivey
Spalding Gray
Dave Barry
Susan Coolidge
Christine O'Keefe Lafser

Genesis 27:27
Barbara Kingsolver
Jodi Picoult
Debra Adelaide
Natalie Angier
George Gordon, Lord
    Byron
Carlos Santana
Katherine Center
Joyce Himnefield
Gwen Stefani
Diana Gabaldon
Nora Okja Keller
Marilyn French
Jiddu Krishnamurti
Mary Karr
Henry David Thoreau
Elizabeth Soutter
    Schwarzer
Edith Willis Linn
Jaroldeen Edwards

ONE & ONLY

Robert Browning
Proverbs 31:28
Oprah Winfrey
Kate Douglas Wiggin
Bolivian proverb
Jewish proverb
N.K. Jemisin

Samuel Taylor Coleridge
William Makepeace
    Thackeray
Keith L. Brooks
Heidi Klum
Adriana Trigiani
Brandi Snyder
T. DeWitt Talmage
Archibald Thompson
Kahlil Gibran
Erica Jong
Diana, Princess of Wales
Adriana Trigiani
Maria Snyder
Mitch Albom
Billy Sunday
Felicia Hemans
Harry Truman
Gaspard Mermillod
Henry Ward Beecher
Louisa May Alcott
Katharine Butler
    Hathaway
Marjorie Holmes
Papiamentu proverb
Nicole Krauss
Margaret Mead
Louisa May Alcott
Thomas Carlyle
Kelly Corrigan

J.K. Rowling
Rudyard Kipling
Megan Mayhew Bergman
Mary Haskell
Alyce Faye Cleese
Arlene Benedict
Valya Dudycz Lupescu
German proverb
Korean proverb
Tatar proverb
Oliver Wendell Holmes Sr.
Marjorie Pay Hinckley
Stasi Eldredge
Felicia Hemans
Spanish proverb

DELIGHT

Muhammad Ali
Pablo Neruda
Mignon McLaughlin
Dr. Sun Wolf
Walt Streightiff
Friedrich Schiller
Eugène Ionesco
Elizabeth Lawrence
Vladimir Nabokov
Cynthia Ozick
Ralph Waldo Emerson
Bill Vaughan
Percy Bysshe Shelley

Mike Mason
Albert Einstein
Douglas Adams
Kirstin Hendrickson
Eileen Kennedy-Moore
Giacomo Leopardi
Cathy Nutbrown
William Wordsworth
D. W. Winnicott
Diane Ackerman
Alice Callahan
Victoria Wagner
J. B. Priestley
Kazuo Ishiguro
Jean-Jacques Rousseau
William Stafford
Hazrat Inayat Khan
Richard Buckminster
  Fuller
Brett Berk
Lev Vygotsky
C. N. Douglas
Rachel Carson
Maurice Sendak
Oliver Wendell Holmes Jr.
Eberhard Arnold
Aldous Huxley
Adam Oehlenschläger
Rainer Maria Rilke

Gretchen Owocki
Christopher Moore
Kelly Corrigan
Tom Stoppard
Marcelene Cox
Kate Greenaway
Charles Lamb
Friedrich Schiller
John Steinbeck
John Betjeman
Lewis Buzbee
Beatrix Potter
John LeCarré
Jane Goodall
Rachel Carson
Ralph Waldo Emerson
Guy de Maupassant
George Santayana
Maria Montessori
Louis de Bernières
Cheryl Dimof
Anna Quindlen
Julian Barnes
Tom Robbins
Eugene Field
Maria Konnikova

HEART

Karl Lagerfeld

Jodi Picoult
Henry David Thoreau
Amy Hatvany
Joan McIntosh
Harlan Coben
Yasmin Le Bon
A. A. Milne
James Joyce
Pema Chodron
Emily Taylor
Erich Fromm
Bess Streeter Aldrich
Charles Dickens
Sister Souljah
American proverb
Neal Shusterman
Nicholas Sparks
Peter Abrahams
Edwin Louis Cole
Honoré de Balzac
Barbra Streisand
Helen Steiner Rice
Washington Irving
Tiffany Baker
Pearl S. Buck
Hamilton Wright Mabie
Arabian proverb
Booth Tarkington
Washington Irving

Kate Samperi
Roald Dahl
Agatha Christie
Jewish proverb
Jane Seymour
Harriet Beecher Stowe
Thomas Aquinas
Penelope Leach
Pramoedya Ananta Toer
Anne Tyler
Marceline Desbordes-
  Valmore
Captain Penny
Jodie Foster
Louisa May Alcott
Osho
C. S. Lewis
Mariama Bâ
Robert Browning
Robert Heinlein

INFLUENCE

Benjamin Spock
Leo Tolstoy
James Baldwin
Anne Morrow Lindbergh
Jim Henson
Walter Landor
Maya Angelou
Michael First

Albert Einstein
Naomi Wolf
Haim Ginott
N. Eldon Tanner
Robert Fulghum
Eleanor Roosevelt
William Feather
Alice Walker
Herbert Spencer
Jean-Jacques Rousseau
Elaine Heffner
Louise Hart
Jeanette Winterson
Zig Ziglar
J. S. Knox
Haim Ginott
Gary Smalley
Walt Whitman
Natalia Ginzburg
Mohandas Gandhi
Eve Merriam
George W. Cecil
Pablo Casals
Charles Alexander
  (Ohiyesa) Eastman
Cathy Warner
  Weatherford
François Rabelais
Robert MacNeil
Tom Sturges
William Shakespeare

George Bernard Shaw
John Lennon
Susan Sarandon
Rabindranath Tagore
Dorothy Canfield Fisher
Abigail Van Buren
Benjamin Franklin
Marc Parent
Elizabeth Gaskell
Mignon McLaughlin
P. D. James
Chinese proverb
Robert Brault
Harry S. Truman
Anne Lamott
John S.C. Abbott
Rosemary Wixom
Jewish proverb
Julianne Moore
Joan Welsh
Andrew Young
Ralph Waldo Emerson
Garrison Keillor
Daphne Kalotay
Phyllis Bottoms
Erma Bombeck
Nicole Johnson
Jonathan Safran Foer
Eileen Kennedy-Moore

TIME

Sister Corita Kent
Evelyn Nown
Karen Joy Fowler
John Bradshaw
Jonathan Tropper
Marc Parent
Jean de La Bruyère
Patricia Clafford
Heather O'Neill
Virginia Woolf
Milli Hill
W. Somerset Maugham
Katrina Kenison
Gail Kelly
Jon Kabat-Zinn
Elizabeth Berg
Elder Neil Andersen
Sarah Napthali
Nancy Woodruff
Orlando A. Battista
Lao Tzu
A. E. Kittredge
Victoria Moran
Heather O'Neill
John Crudele
Takuan Soho
Gretchen Rubin
Gabriela Mistral

Mark Twain
Julie Sokol
Ruth Bell Graham
Dorothy Evslin
Marcelene Cox
Robert Louis Stevenson
Richard Paul Evans
Gregory Maguire
Trisha Ashworth and Amy Nobile
Daniel Gilbert
Rick Warren
Diana Gabaldon
Hillary Rodham Clinton

BALANCE

Rebecca Woolf
Albert Einstein
Milton Berle
Jennifer Crusie
Kate Braverman
Brooke Burke
Elaine Heffner
Pamela Druckerman
Rebecca Woolf
Lotte Bailyn
Rachel Zoe
Oprah Winfrey
Ayelet Waldman
Elif Shafak

Donna Ball
J. K. Rowling
Ann Curry
Kittie Frantz
Sharon Creech
Karen Brown
Meryl Streep
Mary Kay Blakely
Jane Sellman
Miki De Vivo
Susan Lucci
Francine Prose
Ani DiFranco
Andrea Jung
Gwyneth Paltrow
Ann Curry
Elizabeth Blackburn
Rose Kennedy
T. W. Higginson
John Hay
Jodi Picoult
Uma Thurman
Carmen Giménez Smith
Christine Lagarde
Jill Churchill

LAUGH

Julia Louis-Dreyfus
Barbara Schapiro
Phyllis Diller

Kurt Vonnegut Jr.
Ray Romano
Ben Bergor
Robert Gallagher
Benjamin Spock
Jean Kerr
Red Skelton
Amy Poehler
Linda Gerber
Ted Cook
Shannon Fife
Lucie Arnaz
Mark Twain
Sam Levinson
J. D. Salinger
Bill Cosby
Dennis Fakes
Ivan Turgenev
David Frost
Ogden Nash
Ann Diehl
Mona Crane
Erma Bombeck
David Foster Wallace
André Breton
Ed Asner
Michelle Pfeiffer
John Blair Moore
Dorothy DeBolt
Mitch Albom

Lionel Kauffman
Alice Thomas Ellis
Stephanie Pearl-McPhee
Jerry Seinfeld
Bette Davis
Marilyn Penland
Wayne Dyer

GIFTS

Jack Nicholson
Polly Berrien Berends
Fyodor Dostoevsky
Sonia Taitz
C. J. Heck
Liz Armbruster
Kristin Gembala
Henri Frédéric Amiel
Emma Goldman
Franklin P. Jones
Muriel Spark
Gwyneth Paltrow
Tian Dayton
Susannah Martin
Nicole Kidman
Carl Sandburg
Desmond Tutu
Cristina Perez
Marcel Proust
Benjamin Spock
Anne Fadiman

Paulo Coelho
Robert Southey
Susan Wiggs
Nancy Fuchs-Kreimer
Busy Phillips
Yolanda Adams
Ralph Waldo Emerson
Nicola Horlick
Demi Moore
David McArthur
Lisa Wingate
Jon Kabat-Zinn
Robert Brault
Adrianna Lima
Paul Reiser
Thich Nhat Hanh
Angela Carter
Kate Moses
Anne Tyler
Gwyneth Paltrow
Jessica Alba
Erica Jong
Jodie Foster
Debra Messing
Marissa Jaret Winokur
Lily Mae Martin
Madonna
Katherine Ellison
Jada Pinkett Smith
Nancy Pelosi

Cammie McGovern
Kelly Lambert
Pamela Anderson
Angelina Jolie
Laura Schlessinger
Marian Wright Edelman
Peter Krause
Tom Robbins
Joyce Maynard
Sophocles
Angela Schwindt
Eric Hoffer
Robert Brault
Frank A. Clark
Caroline Norton
George Santayana
Agatha Christie
Susie Bright
Leon Blum
Delphine de Girardin

NURTURE

Jim Rohn
Frances Ellen Watkins Harper
Osho
Kathleen Kent
Diane Mariechild
M. Scott Peck

Anna Quindlen
Johann Wolfgang von Goethe
Sinhalese proverb
Louis Cozolino
Jimmy Johnson
Gordon B. Hinckley
Leigh A. Bortins
Maya Angelou
Cokie Roberts
Gerhard Richter
Sandra Sage
Erika Harris
Louann Brizendine
Lao Tzu
Matt Ridley
Sloan Wilson
Brené Brown
E. M. Forster
Henry Ward Beecher
John Lennon
Johann Wolfgang von Goethe
G. K. Chesterton
Garrison Keillor
Jean Vanier
Joyce Brothers
Booker T. Washington
Vimala McClure
Ralph Waldo Emerson

Sophie Jewett
John Holt
Marjorie Pay Hinckley
Denis Waitley
Samantha Bee
Dona Maddux Cooper
Ellenore Angelidis
Lurlene McDaniel
Gladys Hunt
Rowan Coleman

STRENGTH

Marguerite Kelly and Elia Parsons
Barbara Katz Rothman
Roxanne Henke
Amy Leslie
Barbara Kingsolver
Roseanne Barr
Kelly Corrigan
Frank Knox
Tenneva Jordan
E. B. White
Barbara Johnson
Cathy Guisewite
Laura Schlessinger
Tillie Olsen
Sarah Elliot
Adaobi Tricia Nwaubani

Carrie Fisher
Mother Teresa
Jerry Seinfeld
Erma Bombeck
Kristin Hannah
Frank A. Clark
Ariel Swartley
Joseph Morgenstern
Chinese proverb
Ralph Waldo Emerson
Henry Wadsworth
   Longfellow
Honoré de Balzac
Judith Martin
Danielle Steel
Lao Tzu
Victoria Secunda
Plato
Lev Vygotsky
Frank Zappa
Zen saying
"The Golden Girls"
Plutarch
Heidi Klum
Suzanne Collins
Kelly Clayton
Cate Blanchett
Scott Simon
Arianna Huffington
John Steinbeck

Donna Summer
William Ross Wallace
Kamran Pasha
Elizabeth Forsythe Hailey
Tina Fey
Haitian proverb
Richard Kevin Hartley
Muffy Mead-Ferro
Thomas Paine
Buddha
Bill Cosby
Benjamin Spock
Emily James Putnam
Victor Hugo
Stephen King
Katrina Kenison
John Masefield
Alexander Crane
Kate Beckinsale
Creole proverb
Mignon McLaughlin
Sarah Zettel
Victor Hugo
Mitch Albom
Eleanor Roosevelt
James M. Barrie
Nancy Reagan
Helen Hunt
A. A. Milne

PERFECTION

Uma Thurman
Billy Wilder
Mario Andretti
Ralph Ellison
Tiffani Thiessen
Melinda Gates
Sheryl Sandberg
Salvador Dalí
Jessica Alba
Srini Pillay
Erma Bombeck
Nichole Nordeman
Jodi Picoult
Rumi
American proverb
Jane Clayson Johnson
Henry Miller
Ayelet Waldman
Adele Faber
Lionel Shriver
William Shakespeare
Fred Rogers
Maya Angelou
Neil Kurshan
Anthony Robbins
Byron Katie
Nora Roberts
Gretchen Rubin

Alfred, Lord Tennyson
Randy Pausch
Goldie Hawn
Reinhold Niebuhr
Victoria Moran
Dan Millman
Christiane Amanpour
Judsen Culbreth
Rosalynn Carter
Jo-Ann Mapson
Michael Jackson
Jen Lawrence
Simone de Beauvoir
Denis Waitley
Phyllis McGinley
Charles R. Swindoll
Xue Xinran
Rita Mae Brown
Jodi Picoult
Sue Woodman
Carlos Barrios
Emily Watson
Ralph Waldo Emerson
Garrison Keillor
Annie Dillard
Jodi Picoult
Jacqueline Carey
Sherrilyn Kenyon
Anaïs Nin
Dawn Powell

Sarah Dessen
Michael Baron
Lisa Groen Braner
Debby Russell
Lao Tzo
Sue Woodman
Rodolfo Costa
Sheena Iyengar

LIFESAVERS

John Fiebig
Betty Ford
Carol Lin
John Lennon
Jennifer Garner
Robin Grille
Naomi Stadlen
Anna Quindlen
Ric Ocasek
Tina Fey
Rachel Weisz
Lisa Bergren
Dinah Maria Mulock Craik
Samuel Taylor Coleridge
Kristin Hannah
Marcelene Cox
Sandra Steingraber
Saint Augustine
Oprah Winfrey
Jonathan Safran Foer

Jody Watley
Louise Erdich
Cicero
C.S. Lewis
Angela Kinsey
Jim Butcher
Amy Heckerling
Joel Osteen
Theodore Hesburgh
Michael Meyerhoff
Mayim Bialik
Heidi Klum
Sallie Krawcheck
H.R. Schaffer
Jada Pinkett Smith
Margaret Mead
Kurt Vonnegut Jr.
Lisa Bloom
Nancy Pelosi
Carolyn Kepcher
Tina Turner
Bethany Casarjian and
    Diane Dillon
Erica Jong
Louise J. Kaplan
Salma Hayek
Katherine Heigl
Edwidge Danticat
Kongo proverb
Sophie Trudeau

Robert Louis Stevenson
Glenn Close
Janene Wolsey Baadsgaard
Elizabeth Berg
Ursula K. Le Guin
Jane Howard

RENEWAL

Ralph Waldo Emerson
Spanish proverb
Mortimer Adler
William Shakespeare
Pearl S. Buck
Roger Gould
Kathy Ireland
Jack Kornfield
Cindy Crawford
Robyn Sarah
Doris Lessing
Thomas Moore
Amanda Peet
Cate Blanchett
Debra Gilbert Rosenberg
Tori Amos
Lane Olinghouse
Sarah Maizes
Doris Lessing
Doris Mortman
Brooke Castillo
Diane von Furstenberg

Nancy Friday
Penelope Quest
Ron Taffel
Frederick W. Robertson
Confucius

RELEASE

Hodding Carter
Barbara Kingsolver
John Plomp
George Bernard Shaw
William Galvin
Anaïs Nin
Rebecca Richards
Betty Ford
Heather Armstrong
  (Dooce)
Barbara Kingsolver
James M. Barrie
Dorothy Parker
Barbara Delinsky
Owen Meredith
Andrea Richesin
Mitch Albom
Mary Lamb
Tina Fey
F. Scott Fitzgerald
Adam Gopnik
Zig Ziglar
Alison Gopnik

Maureen Wheeler
Nicole Krauss
Lisa See
Lewis Mumford
Theodor Seuss Geisel (Dr.
  Seuss)
Henry Ward Beecher
Sarah Strohmeyer
Toni Morrison

LEGACY

Neil Postman
Alfred North Whitehead
Kahlil Gibran
James Allen
Maxim Gorky
Elie Wiesel
Forest E. Witcraft
Kalu Kalu
Olga Masters
James Griffioen
Chinese proverb
Henry Ward Beecher
Maya Angelou
Halle Barry
Jodi Picoult
Debra Ginsberg
Tina Fey
Anna Quindlen
Daniel Dennett

Curtis Sittenfeld
Salma Hayek
Pablo Picasso
Confucius
Barbara Kingsolver
Cass Elliot
Howard Gardner
Harry Edwards
David Brower
Pope Paul VI
Albert Camus
Orson Scott Card
T.L. Cuyler
Zig Ziglar
Thomas S. Monson
James Baldwin
Montesquieu (Charles-
    Louis de Secondat)
J.R. Miller
Fred Rogers
Mary Steichen Calderone

Charles R. Swindoll
Gordon B. Hinckley
Barbara Kingsolver
Zora Neale Hurston
Barabara Kingsolver
Graycie Harmon
Randy Pausch
Sonia Sanchez
Immanuel Kant
Marc Chagall
Erica Jong
Raffi Cavoukian
Noel Coward
Florida Scott-Maxwell
George Eliot
Thomas A. Edison
Greg Graffin
Franklin D. Roosevelt
Andrew Jackson
Nancy Turner

Shannon Hale
Nancy Friday
C.G. Jung
Alice Walker
Gilda Radner
Stevie Wonder
Johan Wolfgang von
    Goethe
Ellen Goodman
Eileen Kennedy-Moore
Oliver Wendell Holmes Jr.
Carol Lynn Pearson
Julie B. Beck
Anne Frank
Peter Ustinov
Isabel Allende
Mother Teresa
Henry Wadsworth
    Longfellow
Liv Ullmann